Culture
Won

How culture propelled Arm
from start-up to global
technology phenomenon

Keith Clarke

www.culturewon.com

Grosvenor House
Publishing Limited

This book is published by
Grosvenor House Publishing Ltd
Link House
140 The Broadway, Tolworth, Surrey, KT6 7HT.
www.grosvenorhousepublishing.co.uk

A CIP record for this book
is available from the British Library

ISBN 978-1-80381-142-0
eBook ISBN 978-1-80381-143-7

Arm trademark notice

AMBA, Arm, Arm7, Arm7TDMI, Arm9, Arm11, Artisan, big.LITTLE,
CoreLink, Cortex, Ethos, Helium, Jazelle, Keil, Mali, Neon, POP, RealView,
SecurCore, Thumb and TrustZone are trademarks or registered trademarks
of Arm Limited (or its subsidiaries) in the US and/or elsewhere. The related
technology may be protected by any or all of patents, copyrights, designs,
and trade secrets. All rights reserved.

For further information, see:
https://www.arm.com/company/policies/trademarks
Other
All other brands or product names are the property of their respective holders.

For Bryan Clarke, my father, who made a simple request which spurred me into the electronics business – thank you.

For the founders of Advanced RISC Machines, whose passion, hard work, and culture made the extraordinary growth of Arm possible:

John Biggs
Tudor Brown
Pete Harrod
Dave Howard
Harry Meekings
Andy Merritt (sadly deceased)
Mike Muller
Harry Oldham
Sir Robin Saxby
David Seal (sadly deceased)
Lee Smith
Al Thomas (sadly deceased)
Jamie Urquhart

Advanced RISC Machines Limited (latterly **Arm Limited**) was founded in late 1990 as a joint venture with 12 people plus a CEO to develop and monetise the microprocessor technology developed by Acorn Computers Limited. Arm Limited has since become the world's leading semiconductor intellectual property company, with over 5,000 employees from 85+ nationalities. Arm's technologies reach 70% of the global population with an ecosystem of more than 1,000 partners (www.arm.com).

Keith Clarke held numerous senior roles in Arm Limited, having joined the small start-up as an enthusiastic young engineer, employee number 33. In 2018, after 25 years, Keith left to found his coaching and consulting business, **Innovador Limited** (www.innovador-consulting.co.uk), which puts into practice a core truth learned during his time at Arm: that businesses grow when they help people grow. The highly engaging and rewarding work environment of Arm was a large part of what motivated Keith to write this book and the realisation that, very often, the lessons learned at Arm are valid for most enterprises, technology or non-technology.

Contents

Foreword   vii

Preface   ix

Acknowledgements   xi

Introduction   xiii

Arm Timeline   xxi

    One: Find Your Unique   1

    Two: Build Strategy, Test… Repeat   25

    Three: Create and Sustain the Right Culture 55

    Four: Get the Customer's Voice Inside   83

    Five: Build a Delivery Machine   103

    Six: Admit When You're Wrong   129

    Seven: Create an Ecosystem of Shared Success 151

    Eight: Challenge Complacency   171

    Nine: Deal With Threats… Fast   185

    Ten: Stay Unified   213

Afterword   233

Conclusions   235

Appendix   237

Glossary of Terms   243

References   245

Arm Limited Commentary

Acknowledgements

Although this book has been written independently of Arm Limited, I would like to thank the company for its help with historical material and permission to use diagrams and pictures.

Naming Conventions

The original microprocessor technology was called the Acorn RISC Machine, usually shortened to ARM, all uppercase. When the new start-up was spun out, the company name was created to retain the short-form "ARM" by changing "Acorn" to "Advanced", hence Advanced RISC Machines Ltd. At the time of the public share offering in April 1998, the company's name was officially changed to ARM Holdings plc, with ARM Limited as the operating company. Not long after the SoftBank acquisition, a re-branding exercise changed the primary usage to either "arm" or "Arm".

In light of this potential confusion, this book will predominantly use "ARM" to represent Advanced RISC Machines, the middle years of ARM Holdings plc or the early microprocessor technology. I will, however, use "Arm" when talking about the most recent years or the larger historical span.

Foreword

By Sir Robin Saxby, founding CEO of Arm (retired 2007), technology entrepreneur, visiting Professor University of Liverpool. April 2022

Keith has done an excellent job accurately charting the Arm journey and articulating the critical ingredients for Arm's success.

This book is less about what we achieved and more about how we created the right culture alongside the technology and business strategy. The combination led to spectacular growth and industry leadership, making Arm-based microprocessors the most popular on our planet – used in just about every electronic device you can imagine, with over 200 billion Arm-based devices shipped by Arm's semiconductor partners.

I first met Keith after he had been recommended to me by Hermann Hauser, co-founder of Acorn Computers and sponsor of the original ARM processor. At the interview, Keith asked me how we would balance the seemingly conflicting needs of our two major investors: Acorn and Apple. A perceptive question, and we took him on as employee number 33 – he subsequently contributed to the Thumb innovation, and led Engineering and Technical Marketing. Later, when I became President of the IET, he helped me write my Presidential address. Having read the book told through the eyes of Keith, I was pleased and humbled to see the positive impact of the great culture we had created.

While Arm is a technology company, the lessons outlined in this book are almost universally applicable: building an organisation of collaboration, ambition, and innovation. So, whether you are in a start-up, scale-up, or mature business, there is something here for you to take away and apply inside your organisation. As Keith rightly says, this wasn't an easy journey for Arm, but the focus on culture impacted and enabled almost every aspect of the company's performance.

I started working with the Arm founders and investors before the company was created.

I'd known Hermann Hauser before he'd founded Acorn and had partnered with VLSI Technology within my role at ES2. I was aware of the Arm processor through a European project and knew people in Apple. So when a head-hunting phone call from Heidrick and Struggles came in the summer of 1990, I was interested in exploring the possibility of leading the UK headquartered start-up.

My own personal experiences and contacts helped. Without real experience, knowledge has little value. The importance of building trusting relationships and community is often played down, and Keith has done an excellent job bringing about the human factors needed for success.

Through reading the book, I have personally enjoyed refreshing my memory of our journey, both hard and exhilarating. I will personally recommend it to all my friends. Never has humankind needed to collaborate better to save our planet, fix mental health issues, and have a brighter future. I would like to thank all the people of every culture and nationality for contributing to Arm's success, as well as Keith and the other contributors to this outstanding book.

Preface

I started writing this book about Arm in early 2021, inspired by a recent 30th-anniversary 'founders' video call. While the seed for the book had been planted when I left Arm in 2018 after 25 years, seeing and hearing former colleagues and friends vividly reminded me of what this team had helped create. I realised that here was a story that deserved to be told.

Spurred into action, I started collecting material, unsure where it would lead. I reached out to some key figures from Acorn Computers and Arm's early years, including Sophie Wilson, Sir Robin Saxby, and Jamie Urquhart, then started putting 'hand to keyboard'. The purpose soon became clearer: to capture some of what had helped propel Advanced RISC Machines to global success. As the drafts, conversations, and feedback accumulated, the essence became clearer too: Culture.

So, if you are part of any organisation, big or small, commercial or non-commercial, and you want to see your organisation grow and progress, then I believe there is something here for you. The book focuses on the foundational influences that set up the company's direction and the activities that helped evolve those influences into defining characteristics over the following years. I hope you will find something of interest and value here.

Keith Clarke, April 2022

Acknowledgements

Writing a book is rarely possible without lots of help and support, and I am very grateful to all the people who have contributed to this effort in so many ways. There are always too many people to mention all by name, but I will mention a few.

Sir Robin Saxby[1], Advanced RISC Machines' first CEO, provided lots of background on the early development of the business model and strategy. Right from the first call, he encouraged me to tell this story.

Jamie Urquhart, co-implementer of the first ARM processor, ARM founder and past COO, patiently reviewed two different versions of the book. He provided lots of historical detail and candid feedback to help improve the flow and narrative.

John Biggs, ARM founder, opened his ARM historical archive for me and provided details of some of the early stories.

Sophie Wilson, one of the two original ARM processor architects, filled in some missing details from those early years within Acorn, despite being asked to tell the story dozens of times previously.

---

[1] Knighted in the UK 2002 New Year's Honours list

Dave Jaggar, Dave Flynn, and Paul Kimelman, respectively, filled gaps in my knowledge of the Thumb innovation background, synthesisable cores, and the new microcontroller core development.

Bryan Dickman candidly told me what was wrong with an early draft, and finally, Craig Slorach and Ian Thornton contributed significant and helpful review comments.

Introduction

Arm Limited is the world's leading semiconductor Intellectual Property (IP) company. Its extremely power-efficient processor technology has been licensed to hundreds of semiconductor chip manufacturers and Original Equipment Manufacturers (OEMs[2]) – its designs are at the heart of many world-changing technologies. Since its technologies are woven into the fabric of products rather than being a consumer brand in its own right, Arm is still largely unknown to the broader public. Yet Arm's technology is nearly ubiquitous and has been a foundational building block of the global rise of the smartphone and everything this has enabled. Arm-based microprocessors power over 95% of the world's mobile phones.

However, this book is not about the technology. It's about how a company grew from being a small start-up in Cambridge, UK. From 12 people and a £1.75m cash investment in 1990 to a global organisation with over 5,000 employees in over 50 countries and more than $1.5bn revenue in 2016 when SoftBank acquired it for $32bn. This astonishing journey goes back even further, as Acorn Computers Ltd. developed the core microprocessor technology[3] in the mid-1980s. In 1990,

---

[2] OEMs essentially are the companies that bring technologies together to develop a product

[3] Acorn no longer exists but many of its technologies still do

this technology was 'spun out' into a joint venture between Acorn Computers Ltd, Apple Computers Inc.[4] and VLSI Technology Inc.[5]

At the time of the press launch in 1990 of the new company, known then as Advanced RISC Machines, just over 130,000 microprocessor chipsets had been shipped. By 2021, that same number of Arm-based chips was being shipped every three minutes, totalling over 29bn annually. Arm-based processors are by far the highest volume 32-bit/64-bit CPUs shipped in history, with over 200bn cumulatively to date.

Arm's achievements are, therefore, not in doubt. However, not all the reasons for that success are immediately apparent. Some of the more obvious things the company got right include excellent technology, an innovative business model, and perfect timing. However, there is much more to building a world-leading technology business than technology. This book's goal is to peel back some of the outer layers and uncover for the reader more of the less obvious but fundamental reasons that contributed to Arm and its partnerships' ongoing business success.

This book strives to tell some of that less obvious story, honour the people who made a real difference, and help point the way for all organisations (and not just technology companies) who want to create a culture of trust, challenge, and innovation. The observations and conclusions are not definitive, and there is a great deal of room for other perspectives on the Arm story. However, this is my own, hopefully, insightful view as a

---

[4] Renamed Apple Inc.
[5] Now part of NXP Semiconductors N.V.

long-term senior team member who always remained close to the organisation's microprocessor development 'heart'.

It is important to also set the scene by stating that Arm's story is not one of overnight success (although the company was profitable only three years into its life). After ten years, ARM Limited had only 600 employees, and royalty revenues were only recently becoming significant.

Neither was this an easy journey – what Arm achieved has been characterised by solving deeply complex technology and business challenges, one after the other.

What are the essential elements to any organisation's success?

Culture and People?

Strategy?

Execution?

Timing?

Luck?

All undoubtedly play a part.

While the culture of the Acorn engineers provided a solid foundation to build upon, Arm's founders consciously chose the culture they wanted. As the company grew, Arm evolved, but it held onto a culture that supported and encouraged business excellence, minimised positional power and promoted trusting relationships. The capabilities and behaviours of people at Arm made an enormous difference.

The strategy-making process was dynamic, with regular, open, and honest progress reviews, reacting to opportunities and threats with pace.

The execution engine delivered a steady stream of new products and revenue receipts which grew from the founding team's hard-working ethos. At its best, Arm delivered multiple years of quarterly financial results meeting or exceeding analysts' expectations. We built an operational machine to be proud of.

Timing played a pivotal role in Arm's success, with the foundational business strategy taking advantage of the perceived opportunities for a licensable microprocessor in the semiconductor industry. The early 1990s saw the exponential rise of System on Chip designs using embedded microprocessors, significantly validating Arm's business model.

As with every successful organisation, luck did play a part. Perhaps it was luck that Acorn had fewer resources than their international competitors, leading them to build a new microprocessor using very few resources. The result was an extremely small, strongly performing 32-bit processor that consumed very little power. When almost everyone else was trying to maximise performance, Acorn tried to maximise power efficiency. This 'luck' was turned into an asset that Advanced RISC Machines was able to embed in its DNA thoroughly. Another piece of 'luck' was that Acorn had licensed the processor to their chip manufacturer, VLSI Technology Inc., who were allowed to sell it to other customers too. Acorn's early interest had been in computers, not the Intellectual Property itself – Advanced RISC Machines were then able to take advantage of that early validation of IP licensing and turn it into a business model. Arm's culture and strategy enabled the organisation to take advantage of unexpected opportunities as they arose – call it Entrepreneurial Alertness (Kirzner, 2018) or luck, whichever you prefer.

Success for any organisation will combine all elements, not in an additive way but a multiplicative way. Every element: culture and people, strategy, execution, timing and luck, must be at least good enough; when combined, the result should be excellent outcomes. In Arm's case, I believe that Culture and People were the foundation on which the other success factors were built. Arm's strategy and execution (and, to a degree, luck) have been excellent, primarily due to the organisation's cultural norms. Putting to one side elements like timing and luck, we might say that the success equation became:

$$Success = Culture^2 \times Strategy \times Execution$$

Culture permeated so much of what Arm has been able to achieve.

If you want to find a champion of culture in your organisation, then a great place to look is yourself. If you want to see appropriate behaviours, you could start to model them and encourage others to do the same. An organisation's authentic culture is the one acted day-in, day-out by colleagues, not necessarily the ones on a poster next to the coffee machines!

In this book, I hope to give some insight into what I believe are the essential ingredients in Arm's success: ten areas covering the elements of culture and people, strategy, execution, and more. How were these chosen? Some were clear from the outset, but others rose in prominence as I began researching and writing. Like any organisation, the recipe for success will have many ingredients – I believe these ten steps to success, illustrated by Arm's experiences, will be relevant to almost any organisation with ambitions for growth. There is no guaranteed way to make a success of a venture, but by understanding some of the how, why, and what behind Arm's journey, I hope the book will inspire you to ensure your recipe has many of the best ingredients, mixed carefully to provide the best possible outcomes.

A Note on the Book Structure

I have written this as a business book for entrepreneurs, leaders of start-ups, scale-ups, organisations with growth ambitions, and those interested in the story of Arm. There is necessarily some technology talk – to help, I've written a short Industry and Technology Context section in the Appendix. If you're unfamiliar with the technology space, read this first, as I hope you will find this helps to explain the context of Arm's business. You may find it somewhat simple if you're familiar with this space. You can also see a glossary of terms at the back to help with the technical terminology.

With ten chapters, I realise that the reader may be interested in some topics more than others, so you may choose to read only those of immediate interest or in a different order. Each chapter is reasonably standalone, though there is some chronological order to the first two to three chapters. The first chapter primarily covers the historical background of Acorn and the assets that arose from the early Acorn activities. If you're less interested in that historical context, then perhaps start at Chapter 2, where the focus is more on the Arm situation, with occasional references to the foundations laid by Acorn's and Robin Saxby's experiences.

I have written the chapters in the style of steps needed by an organisation to create a successful outcome. I'm not claiming these steps are easy to achieve, but almost anything is possible with the right mindset of total honesty, collaboration, planning, execution, and continuous refinement.

1. **Find your Unique** – A historical look at the foundational assets of Advanced RISC Machines Limited

2. **Build Strategy, Test… Repeat** – Building the initial business plan and strategy, and then further Arm refinement

3. **Create and Sustain the Right Culture** – Creating and evolving the culture of Arm

4. **Get the Customer's Voice Inside** – Ensuring Arm heard and acted upon outside voices

5. **Build a Delivery Machine** – Building an operational machine to deliver new products and revenue consistently

6. **Admit When You're Wrong** – Fighting against Arm's common wisdom

7. **Create an Ecosystem of Shared Success** – Building a partnership with the industry for mutual benefit

8. **Challenge Complacency** – Keeping the pace and expectations high

9. **Deal With Threats… Fast** – Reacting with pace to outside threats and competitive products

10. **Stay Unified** – Staying united despite growth and diversification

Arm Timeline

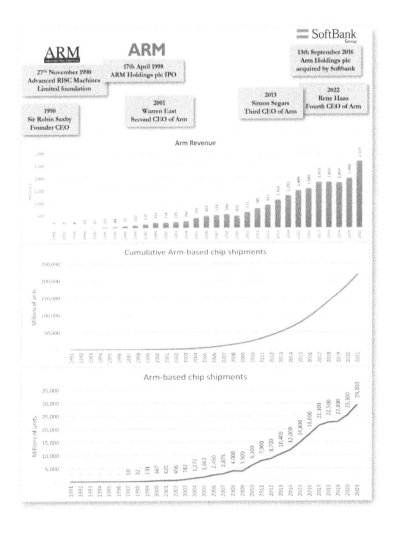

One: Find Your Unique

When James Dyson set up Dyson Appliances Limited in 1991, he had no intention of bringing a standard vacuum cleaner to market. Inspired by giant cyclone technology in a factory setting, thousands of prototypes later, Dyson started selling the dual-cyclone bagless vacuum cleaner from his own company. He founded the business on a technology unique in the consumer market, and within a few years, the best-selling vacuum cleaner in the UK was the Dyson DC01. His determination to bring something unique and valuable to the market paid off (Dyson-Various, 2022), and Dyson's products have become synonymous with doing things differently.

If you had asked the founders of Advanced RISC Machines what made them unique in 1990, you would have heard the following: small, embeddable, and power-efficient microprocessor technology, plus an enthusiastic and talented technical team with broad computer systems experience. These were the seeds of the company's eventual success; the story would have been very different without them. The technology itself looks very simple from a modern perspective, but as far as many inside Acorn Computers were concerned, the crown jewels were given away to the new start-up.

The Acorn RISC Machine (ARM) microprocessor, software and systems IP were the technology seed at the heart of the new start-up, Advanced RISC Machines Limited, founded on 27th November 1990. Acorn's contribution to the joint venture was the technology and 12 engineers. Apple Computers Inc. and VLSI Technology Inc. completed the assets of the new enterprise with modest financial investments. Apple wanted to use the microprocessor in a future product, not having its own CPU design capability. VLSI Technology had been the first manufacturer of Acorn's chipsets and had seen an opportunity to sell more devices using ARM technology. Advanced RISC Machines was created to ensure the survival and continued development of the ARM processor technology when Acorn was struggling to fund its development.

The launch press release outlines their public-facing goals: "expand ARM technology product offerings and to promote other sources to support the expanding customer base" (Press Release, 1990). There was a clear desire to expand the products and customers widely. No other organisation had this mix of licensable, low-power, and power-efficient RISC microprocessor technology (see Appendix), computer systems engineering know-how, and global ambition. Despite their modest resources – it was indeed a unique proposition. However, there were no guarantees they could monetise this proposition beyond their investors and initial customers: Acorn and Apple.

Like all the crucial elements of Arm's eventual success, building a unique and valuable technology wasn't simple. The birth of the technology was rooted in a small team within Acorn Computers Limited, founded in Cambridge, UK, in the late 1970s. To understand the uniqueness of the Acorn technology and the founding team, let's go back to the beginnings, well before Advanced RISC Machines' foundation.

Acorn Computers Limited

The early days of Acorn are notable for their impact on later technology decisions and the healthy working culture that the founders of Advanced RISC Machines largely inherited. So, it's worth recounting some of the critical events of Acorn, the story which the BBC docudrama "The Micro Men" most famously told (Metzstein, 2009). More details with less drama can be found in interviews with some of the people of those early days (Hauser, 2014), (Curry, 2016), (CACM, 2011), (Wilson, 2012). In this book, we'll pull out some of the most relevant points only. The purpose is to understand the foundations that led to the ARM processor and Advanced RISC Machines several years later.

Hermann Hauser and Chris Curry set up Cambridge Processor Unit Ltd. (CPU) in late 1978, having been fascinated by the possibilities of microprocessors (Hauser, 2018). Hermann described the belief that microprocessors would change the world (Manners, 2001). They looked in the Cambridge University Processor Group for talent and found both Steve Furber and Sophie Wilson – whose professional partnership went on to conceive and implement the Acorn RISC Machine processor.

The company won a contract to build a microprocessor-based controller for a fruit machine, using a National Semiconductor SC/MP processor system built by Steve, the MK14 (CACM, 2011). When Sophie looked at Steve's MK14 system, according to Steve, she commented, "I can do better than that" – the first of many occasions. While still an undergraduate, she created a system using a MOS Technology 6502 microprocessor over the Easter holidays, which Hermann thought was good enough to sell as a kit alongside Steve's MK14. They chose the trading name Acorn Computers Limited to sell the kits. Steve designed the cassette interface, and the Acorn System 1 was launched, targeting semi-professional users and serious home enthusiasts.

The choice of the 6502 microprocessor was to be a significant factor in the later development of the Acorn RISC Machine. It was an 8-bit CPU designed to be simpler, lower cost, and higher performance than Motorola's 6800 or Intel's 8080. The price and simplicity of processors such as the 6502 inspired people worldwide to experiment with microprocessor systems. In the USA, Steve Wozniak was a hobbyist who built computers using the 6502, eventually leading to the Apple II computer (Wozniak, 1977). Apple's shared 6502 roots likely led to its admiration for the ARM processor many years later.

CPU Ltd. continued to develop the microcomputer kits, turning some of these into kits for customers under the Acorn brand. Chris Curry wanted to build a complete computer directly for home enthusiasts. In March 1980, they launched the Acorn Atom with an all-in-one package recognisable from almost all home microcomputers of the early 1980s. It sold an impressive (for the time) 12,000 units, but Sophie recalls she didn't think much of the design: chips would fall out of the circuit board if you typed too enthusiastically on the keyboard (Wilson, 2012).

This dissatisfaction, "I can do better than that", was a hallmark of Sophie, Steve, and many other Acorn engineers. This culture continued through Acorn and into Advanced RISC Machines many years later. They didn't like the Atom's lack of expandability. When Professor Andy Hopper from Cambridge

University suggested they build workstations with higher performance, it was clear something new would be required.

Hermann allowed the team to design an alternative, the Proton, with expansion capability, allowing future (more capable) processors to be attached through a second processor interface. However, he insisted the new base design was still based on the 6502 to keep costs under control. These decisions proved very fortunate, firstly for what happened next, and secondly for the future development of the ARM processor.

"I can do better than that"

The British Broadcasting Corporation

Early in 1980, the BBC[6] wanted to create a TV series to promote computer literacy. Through the involvement of the British government, the idea was born to develop a British computer to go with the programmes. After initially selecting a machine from another organisation, it became clear this wasn't going to be ready for the series due to start in Autumn 1981. The BBC then allowed other companies to bid for the contract.

According to Sophie (Wilson, 2012), Chris said to the BBC: "Well, why don't you come and see the prototype we're making?" Unfortunately, there was no actual prototype, just some sketches and ideas. Sophie and Steve had been discussing the Proton design for some time, but now Hermann and Chris

---

[6] the UK's public service broadcaster

needed action. Time for a bit of subterfuge in the assistance of making progress.

On that fateful Sunday evening, Hermann phoned up Steve and asked whether there was any chance of having a prototype by Friday for a demonstration. Hermann recalled that Steve responded, "No, absolutely not. This is a crazy idea." (Cowley, 2022). Nonetheless, Hermann then called Sophie and told her that Steve had said it might be possible if they worked really hard. Sophie responded that this was mad, but if Steve was willing to try, then so was she. To complete the circle, all that remained was for Hermann to call Steve back to tell him Sophie had said it was possible.

Of course, they quickly discovered Hermann's ruse on Monday morning, but it was too late by then. They knew it was the right thing to try, so they did, along with a core team of engineers. Monday and Tuesday to draw schematics and obtain scarce parts such as high-performance memory chips. Wednesday to wire wrap 3,000 connections, and Thursday to debug it. By 2am Friday, the connections seemed correct, but it still wasn't working properly. With the software still to port, Sophie went home to sleep and arrived back at 8am to find the team sleeping on the floor and the hardware system magically working (Wilson, 2021). Hermann's role as cheerleader and tea maker had been upgraded when he suggested they disconnect the debug system they were using to programme it remotely. Despite the engineers' protests, this worked; then, as Hermann and Chris delayed the BBC downstairs, Sophie ported BASIC[7] and some of the operating system, hacked the video into life,

---

[7] BASIC was a popular programming language of that era

and had a very simple line drawing demonstration working when they came in.

With a mix of the right skills and intense collaboration, this can-do attitude had built the prototype Chris had promised in only four-and-a-half days. The BBC team had no idea of the behind-the-scenes efforts and were impressed with what they saw. Shortly afterwards, the BBC awarded the contract to Acorn, and the "BBC Micro" was launched in December 1981 (BBC Micro, 1981) with a range of innovative features. Sophie and Steve thought the BBC Micro was just half of the system they had set out to build, the 6502-based I/O[8] controller. The design included an interface to allow second processors to be attached, which gave the potential for the workstations that Andy Hopper had asked them to build. The simple "I/O controller", the BBC Micro, went on to sell a million-and-a-half units versus the few thousands they had imagined.

BBC Microcomputer launched in 1981

There are three key things to pull out here for the story of Advanced RISC Machines' founding assets.

---

[8] Input and Output

The first is the initial thought process: they wanted a better CPU than the 6502 for the future, hence the second processor interface. They designed the Proton and then the BBC Micro with this expandability in mind.

The second is equally important but was less evident at the time. The specification agreed with the BBC was designed to appeal to a wide range of users and contained some complex elements. To reduce the manufacturing cost, they needed some semi-custom designed chips, called Uncommitted Logic Arrays (ULAs). This requirement gave the team experience building computer systems from catalogue chips, plus building, albeit simple, chip designs. It was a bold and unusual move for a small company like Acorn, but it proved to be a valuable experience.

Finally, and related, the Acorn engineers were designing the whole computer system around the CPU. This gave them more freedom and flexibility to optimise the system, and it's the vantage point from which they started their journey towards the Acorn RISC Machine.

Acorn's initial commercial success with the BBC Micro enabled the team to start investigating options for future processors with more performance than the 6502. They used the second processor capability of the BBC Micro to analyse many of the then available microprocessors and found as many limitations. They wanted the best elements of the 6502 (simplicity, low cost, and fast interrupt response) but with increased address space and wider datapaths to give the performance they wanted.

Apple was, at the time, a competitor in the education market, and their early 1983 launch of the Lisa computer showed that a graphics interface was going to be vital for future microcomputers too. Sophie and Steve were beginning to feel a new processor architecture might be needed if they were to build the computer they wanted. They wanted a 16 or 32-bit CPU that was easy to program and had some particular technical characteristics[9]. They could not find a commercially available microprocessor that provided all of these – and none of the RISC processors were yet available outside their development labs. When they asked for special samples of the 80286 processor, Intel refused (Engadget, 2011). Perhaps, this is something Intel may have regretted some years later.

MIPS[10] for the Masses

One common feature of many of the microprocessors they tested was their complex instruction sets. However, the RISC movement was underway: Steve remembers Hermann talking about the RISC idea after a business trip to the US, and Sophie remembers Andy Hopper putting copies of the Berkeley RISC (Patterson & Sequin, A VLSI RISC, 1982) and Stanford MIPS (Stanford MIPS, 1983) papers on her desk to read shortly after they were published.

University research teams had created these simpler designs with the same or better performance than commercial microprocessors available at the time. This information was the inspiration Sophie and Steve needed. Sophie set about tinkering with a new instruction set using RISC principles and the knowledge they learned from all that was good about the 6502's efficiency, her "I can do better than that" instinct coming to the

---

[9] very good interrupt response and efficient use of memory

[10] Millions of Instructions Per Second (MIPS)

fore. With no RISC processors available to trial, the only option was to build one themselves.

They had previously visited a National Semiconductor design centre in Israel and found a large team designing a processor, but in October 1983, they had an epiphany. They visited the Western Design Center (WDC) office in Phoenix, Arizona, where Bill Mensch[11] was building a successor to the 6502. They found Bill with a couple of interns doing most of the work. On leaving their office, Steve remembers the conversation: "Well, if they can design a microprocessor, so can we." (CACM, 2011). They realised how few resources might be needed if the design was kept very simple.

Sophie's tinkering solidified into a 32-bit RISC-based instruction set and a behavioural model written in 6502 machine code. Acorn's vision was 'MIPS for the masses' (Wilson, 2012) – a highly efficient processor using readily available memory to deliver high performance at an affordable price. This desire to build a mid-range computer set them on a different path from most workstation-focused alternatives emerging from the US in the 1980s.

The Acorn RISC Machine project was officially given the go-ahead in October 1983 in great secrecy, with each "project A" team member receiving a personal letter reminding them of the need for complete confidentiality. Acorn had grown very quickly to 100s of employees based on the success of the BBC Micro and had recently raised capital with a share flotation. However, Hermann ensured this team had to design an efficient processor because he gave them "no money" and "no people"

---

[11] Co-designer of the original MOS Technology 6502

(Hauser, 2018). This hyperbole, often told by Hermann, wasn't true, of course, but relative to many other high-performance processor development teams, Acorn's approach was indeed miserly. This is not surprising: during 1984, Acorn's financial troubles had begun – the bubble was starting to burst on the home computer revolution.

Keep It Simple, Stupid (KISS)

As the project got underway, Steve then wrote a hardware level emulator of the pipelined processor in BBC BASIC that was compared to Sophie's models for consistency. Next, this Register Transfer Level (RTL) digital design had to be turned into real transistor circuits and chip layout.

With the team's early experience with custom ULAs for the BBC and Andy Hopper's encouragement to get serious about computer design, Acorn had invested in a limited set of chip design tools: Apollo workstations and tools from semiconductor manufacturer VLSI Technology. Acorn recruited a small team of experienced, full-custom integrated circuit designers (VLSI engineers), starting with Robert Heaton and Jamie Urquhart (Urquhart, 2021). The overall team was small but highly motivated, with a strong desire to make what resources they had work. Building a software emulator was merely the first of many home-grown tools the team created to get the job done.

The team ploughed forward, believing that they would run into trouble at some point. However, no significant roadblocks were found. As Steve described, "It turned out, there is no magic. Microprocessors are just a lump of logic, like everything else we'd designed, and there are no formidable hurdles." The RISC philosophy of simple instructions led to a relatively simple design.

Sophie's instruction set was complete in December 1983, and 15 months after the project go-ahead, on a snowy day in January 1985, they hand-delivered a tape containing the full transistor layout to VLSI Technology's office in Munich.

The first ARM processor used a 3μm process and was only 25,000 transistors. In contrast, Intel's 80286 with 134,000 transistors, introduced four years earlier, had lower performance. Even Berkeley's RISC-I was nearly double the Acorn RISC Machine at 44,500 transistors (Peek, 1983).

Three months later, on 26th April 1985, they plugged the chip into a waiting development board. Two hours later, at 3pm, it started to execute instructions spitting out the obligatory "Hello world." Nearly all the instructions operated precisely as desired on first-time silicon – a minor barrel shifter issue was worked around in software (Urquhart, 2021). This feat may not seem remarkable, but the primitive nature of the tools and difficulty of verification led other contemporary projects to take many silicon iterations.

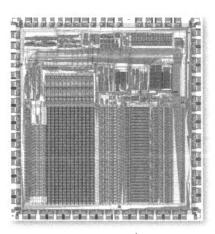

First ARM1 silicon: 26th April 1985

Champagne bottles were at the ready and popped in celebration – a tradition Hermann encouraged and continued well into the early years of Advanced RISC Machines. The next step was to measure the power consumption. As Steve started to attach an ammeter to the power pin, he discovered the power wasn't connected! The processor was pulling all the power it needed from the tiny amount provided through the I/O pins – to spell this out: this was a very low power processor.

When I asked Sophie what she considered the most important technical features to achieve efficiency and low power, she answered, "Nothing more than KISS" (Wilson, 2021). With simplicity, everything else followed. With this simplicity and meticulous VLSI techniques, it was possible to achieve high performance with low area and power (Urquhart, 2021).

The small hardware design team of Sophie, Steve, Robert, and Jamie had built a 32-bit processor with just the features and capabilities they felt necessary to achieve their goals. Almost by accident, they had endowed the processor with power efficiency and low power consumption, which were the defining technical advantages for Advanced RISC Machines' products in years to come.

Acorn aimed to build a home, educational, and business computer with the ARM processor to replace the BBC Micro. The team needed to slightly enhance the first ARM design and design peripheral chips to realise their complete plan. They were able to complete their simulations of the new chips using ARM-based second processors! The first full product was the Acorn Archimedes, launched in mid-1987 using four custom chips: ARM2 (processor), VIDC (display), MEMC (memory), and

IOC (I/O). The Archimedes was the world's first RISC processor-based home computer and claimed to be its fastest, too (Acorn RISCs it, 1987).

From Acorn to Advanced RISC Machines

The arrival of the Acorn Archimedes was a significant milestone for the ARM processor – here it was, finally being used for its intended purpose: 'MIPS for the masses'. The Acorn Archimedes was one of the fastest home and educational computers available at launch. It was a fantastic step forward for those of us who had grown up on the BBC Micro and were loyal to the brand. This computer was the "BBC Micro on steroids", with many Acorn fans jumping on board.

Unfortunately, the leap in performance wasn't enough to take on the march of both Apple Macintosh and IBM PC compatibles. Although Acorn would go on to sell over 500,000 units by 1996 (ART, 1996), in 1989, they were still only selling a few tens of thousands a year. The original Archimedes machines only had a simple operating system: Arthur[12]. The fully graphical operating system it deserved didn't arrive until 1989 in the form of RISC-OS. This delay slowed initial sales, and Acorn's financial performance was poor – they needed to expand beyond educational computers. The Advanced Research & Development (AR&D) group, who had designed the Acorn RISC Machine, the peripheral chips, and the early development computers, looked like an expensive overhead.

Alarm bells were ringing among many at Acorn who saw the ARM processor as a jewel in the crown. If only they could find

---

[12] Archimedes OS by Thursday

a way of saving the technology and the expertise. It was clear to Steve and others that funding further development of the ARM technology would require new markets to be found. Steve described how he tried three times to work out a business model to save the technology (CACM, 2011): "We needed a bigger market, so I tried to work out how to spin out a company. I could never get the numbers to work. You have to sell millions before the royalties start paying the bills. We couldn't imagine selling millions of these things, let alone billions."

By 1989 Malcolm Bird had arrived as Technical Director of Acorn. He pulled together another business plan in an attempt to save the team and its technology. Acorn had already licensed the processor to VLSI Technology, so the business plan suggested that a spin-out company take the technology and license it further, perhaps with some consulting services. There had already been some other interest in using the technology outside of Acorn, including Hermann's new venture, the Active Book Company (ABC). ABC built a chip (Hercules) using the ARM processor as the basis for its prototype hand-held computer (Active-Book, 1988).

However, there were no clear high-volume opportunities, and the future still looked uncertain – that was about to change as interest arrived from another source.

The Apple Factor

The Apple II, based on the 6502, had been selling since 1977, having been upgraded and extended along the way. The 1984 Apple Macintosh used Motorola's 68000, leaving some inside Apple wanting to investigate alternative processors for the future. Two members of Apple's Advanced Technology Group

(ATG) had spotted the ARM processor, rightly inferring the 6502 heritage and inspiration (Nenni & Dingee, 2015).

They had initially bought an ARM reference system. Later, during the 2-year Möbius project, they created a system using VLSI Technology's ARM2-based chip with software to emulate the Apple II and the Apple Macintosh. They found they could emulate running the native software quicker than the original machines – quite an achievement. After presenting their results to the rest of ATG, the project was shut down – possibly because it was a distraction.

In the meantime, development had started elsewhere in ATG on the Newton project to create a new product category: the "Personal Digital Assistant" (PDA), a small handheld device. Apple, at that time, had no capability to build a microprocessor, so it had funded the development of a RISC-inspired processor[13] at AT&T for this purpose (Tesler, 1999). The programme ran into cost challenges, and the processor was not delivering the necessary performance or features. Larry Tesler[14] was now in charge of ATG and the Newton development. He needed a solution to quickly turn around the project's fortunes. Larry had seen the ATG presentation of the ARM processor results, and VLSI Technology's John Stockton was promoting the use of the ARM processor to companies in Silicon Valley (Saxby, 2021). Larry met Hermann Hauser when the latter was touring the US promoting the Active Book project. Although VLSI Technology was selling the ARM processor chips, Larry didn't feel Apple could rely on technology owned by a small British computer company. Though no longer part of Acorn,

---

[13] later known as 'Hobbit'

[14] Larry Tesler was a senior executive at Apple at the time

Hermann was well aware of the need to find a business opportunity for the team. He proposed a joint venture solution to Larry, and they brainstormed what it might look like (Urquhart, 2021).

Hermann then brokered a meeting between Larry and Malcolm Bird, and soon a group of Apple engineers was flying to Cambridge, UK, on a fact-finding mission. The visit was a resounding success. They saw the potential of the technology to provide the necessary high-performance and low-power they needed for the Newton.

The Formation of Advanced RISC Machines

The two companies had enough interest in common to make this work: Apple wanted a CPU built for its Newton project, and Acorn wanted to divest from the future development costs while keeping the technology alive. They hammered out a joint venture agreement with a provisional start date before the end of 1990, with VLSI Technology Inc. making up the third partner. All that was missing were the 'trivial' matters of selecting which team members would move to the new entity, choosing the IP and assets to transfer, and needing a Chief Executive. And, of course, the creation of a viable business plan.

Malcolm Bird, Sophie Wilson, and Jamie Urquhart, with input, carefully chose the founding 12 engineers from Acorn's AR&D team (Urquhart, 2021). Steve Furber had already taken up a post at the University of Manchester, UK, and Sophie preferred to stay with Acorn, so neither moved to ARM. Some of the selected 12 felt relieved to be saved from Acorn. Others thought they were being pushed out and were unwanted. Dave

Howard recalled discovering the proposed joint venture on return from a summer holiday in 1990 (Howard, 2021). Although he was sceptical about the idea, he knew it was better to stay as a team and face the new challenges together.

They were a tight-knit team with a can-do attitude and were not short on engineering talent and ingenuity. However, none of the team had any significant commercial or executive-level experience. An outside CEO was one of the requirements of the investors. The recruitment started well before the foundation day to ensure the new company had the necessary business leadership. Heidrick and Struggles were employed to conduct an executive search, leading to Sir Robin Saxby being head-hunted from ES2. After working out his notice, he would join full time in February 1991, although he had agreed to work 50-50 for the transition period (Saxby, 2021).

Most of the team shared a strong desire to make something of the technology and not repeat some of Acorn's commercial mistakes. Their spirit of collaboration, invention, determination, and their share of luck, would eventually propel the new company way beyond their expectations.

Advanced RISC Machines Holdings Limited Foundation

On 27th November 1990, Advanced RISC Machines Holdings Limited was born. They chose the name to retain the acronym ARM from the original Acorn RISC Machine. The selected 12 engineers and the ARM technology were Acorn's contribution to the company's assets. Apple contributed £1.5m cash for an equal share of ownership with Acorn. VLSI Technology Inc. contributed £250k and EDA development tools for their initial

CPU licence and minority share. Employee shares made up the remainder. Robin chose a holdings board management structure with the investors' directors, insulating this from the operating company to prevent operational leaks. This structure proved valuable in later years when ARM wanted to introduce the Thumb® technology against Acorn's wishes.

Team Culture

Although Sophie and Steve are most closely associated with the design of the Acorn RISC Machine processor, there were many others instrumental in the full development of the Acorn Archimedes computer. Acorn had assembled an expanded team of system designers, software and VLSI engineers – many of whom would go on to be part of AR&D and eventually be founders of Advanced RISC Machines.

So, what were the defining characteristics of this team?

By the mid-1980s, it was possible to design bespoke silicon chips and have them manufactured, just as the Acorn RISC Machine was crafted. The instruction set defines the architecture, followed by a digital logic design to implement that architecture accurately. The original logic designer, Steve, was joined by Tudor Brown, Al Thomas, Mike Muller and, later, Pete Harrod. The latter four were eventual co-founders of Advanced RISC Machines. The digital logic was then turned into transistor circuits that faithfully implemented the logic design. The latter task was the role of Acorn's VLSI engineers, such as Robert Heaton, who led that team initially. He worked with Jamie, who was later joined by his ex-colleagues from Plessey, Dave Howard and Jim Sutton. After Robert left, John Biggs and Harry Oldham joined the team, with Jamie becoming the team leader. Jamie, Dave, John, and Harry became the founding VLSI team of Advanced RISC Machines.

The engineers established a highly collaborative environment to ensure the ideas conceived early in the design process were capable of being implemented efficiently in the silicon design. For example, when Sophie was considering an instruction set with the ability to shift values before an operation (a barrel shifter), Steve had to ascertain whether or not it was possible to implement this feature in a single clock cycle. Robert and Jamie built some test circuits and layouts to demonstrate the feasibility.

The simplicity of design was vital – it would have been easy to create a design that needed more circuit and layout resources than were available. The tools of that time were primitive relative to modern expectations, and they built a lot of their own. For example, they wrote a tool for statically checking the timing of circuits: STCalc; and a tool to automatically generate specific types of logic decoders: PLAGen (Biggs, 2021). The culture was one of DIY where no alternatives existed – anything to get a simple design that worked.

Committing to manufacturing a prototype chip in those days could cost tens of thousands of dollars and a few months turn-around – so before creating a tape of instruction files for the manufacturer, the engineers had to have very high confidence in the design. Hence a lot of simulation was needed to check the digital logic performed as expected, and that the layout of transistors and connections faithfully implemented that digital logic at the target frequency speed.

The team had grown in size since the original Acorn RISC Machine. Still, the attention to detail, the collaborative working practices, the careful processes, and the DIY attitudes were the glue that kept them effective and successful. The original ARM design had given them confidence, too. They knew that they could build the chips and the computer system they wanted with teamwork and care. When they looked at what they saw elsewhere, they thought, "We can do better than that."

This confidence was also rooted in the knowledge that they had each other's backs. To ensure the transistor level implementations were a correct representation of the digital logic was not easy – there were no comparison tools available at the time. Robert instituted a set of processes and practices to help give confidence and assurance (Urquhart, 2021). There were rigorous protocols, and a design flow focused on intermediate test points to compare the design at different levels with joint accountability. They also encouraged the constant improvement of design and validation processes. There was a concerted effort to avoid over-specialisation in such a small team, dynamically moving people to gain more experience and propagate new ideas. A culture of cross-checking and reviewing each other's work ensured tight collaboration of the system designers with Acorn's VLSI engineers.

Advanced RISC Machines' Assets

Soon after the foundation, as part of the ongoing formulation of the business plan and strategy, Robin asked Jamie to perform a Strengths, Weaknesses, Opportunities, and Threats (SWOT) analysis with the whole ARM team. Think of this as a strategic asset stocktake.

ARM LTD SWOT   18.12.90   CONFIDENTIAL

STRENGTHS:

Basic Technology: low power
                                 low cost (component & system)
                                 simple
                                 small

Established Team: flexible
                                 responsive
                                 dynamic
                                 successful (so far)
                                 enthusiastic
                                 extensive systems experience

WEAKNESSES:

Poor Comercial Starting Point: market share
                                 market profile
                                 revenue
                                 marketing expertise

Limited Resources

Third Party Support :   ICE / logic analyser
                                 cross compiler
                                 HDL
                                 technical support

Characterisation & Test

Reliance upon Foundry

OPPORTUNITIES:

Emerging Markets (applications) portables
                                 embedded control
                                 automotive
                                 rad-hard
                 (places)   : Japan / Far East
                                 Europe
                                 OMI / ESA

Partnerships: Silicon Manufacturers
                                 Silicon Users
                                 Silicon Distributers

Apple

Consultancy

THREATS:

Big Rivals

Patents   own   none.

Small team - reliance upon individuals

Existing Commitments - yielding low revenue

Single Customer at present

No Control over Income

The 18th December 1990, SWOT Analysis

The strengths identified tell a story of their technology inheritance and their view of themselves:

- **Technology**: Low power, Low cost, Simple, Small

- **Team**: Flexible, Responsive, Dynamic, Successful, Enthusiastic, Systems experience

The legacy of Acorn's Project A had endowed them with a small and low power microprocessor. The 12-person team comprised a healthy balance of skills: four system designers, four software and algorithms engineers, and four VLSI engineers. Together they had designed and built complete computer systems, and they had had a lot of technical success building their bespoke silicon chips. The twists and turns of Acorn's fortunes meant they had needed to grow flexibility and determination too.

Looking back over 30 years later, it's perhaps slightly easier to assess the unique set of skills and critical assets the new organisation had:

1) Small, power-efficient, and low-power RISC microprocessor technology

2) Licensable and embeddable microcell for System-on-Chip designs

3) Full computer system expertise

4) Experienced, collaborative, successful, and determined team

5) Experienced and commercially focused CEO

6) Acorn and Apple's sponsorship and validation.

The Weaknesses and Opportunities of the SWOT show a final key element of what was to serve Advanced RISC Machines exceptionally well in the future. The group was all too aware that they had minimal resources: 12 engineers, a CEO, and £1.75m of start-up funding. In turning the thought process upside down, it's possible to see how their lack of resources yet desire to proliferate the technology led to the final piece of the puzzle: the strategy and business proposition that helped make Advanced RISC Machines unique. In the next chapter, we'll explore the development and evolution of the global licensing business model, the development of the new business goals, and the action plans to achieve them, i.e., strategy planning.

Chapter Summary and Lessons

The journey of the key players and the technology had taken a little over ten years to move from the "I can do better than that" Acorn System 1 through the design of a completely new processor architecture to the foundation of Advanced RISC Machines. Not all new ventures start with such a long lead time, but all begin with tangible and intangible assets. At the foundation of ARM, the team had an honest assessment of their assets and capabilities to create some clarity on what unique benefits they could bring to the market. The microprocessor technology had a unique combination of capabilities, but this wasn't enough. That technology, with the right team culture, skills, and an appropriate business model, amounted to something of real value on which a business could be built.

Whether you are involved in an existing organisation or a start-up hoping to build a sustainable business, spending time to assess what are your critical assets (technology, services, people, customers, and so on) will enable you to answer the crucial question: "What's your unique?"

Two: Build Strategy, Test… Repeat

At its simplest, strategy is a plan of action designed to achieve a goal. In business, it's about making choices, often with uncertain information, based on your current knowledge of the market and the resources you can assemble. When Apple brought the first iPhone™ to market in 2007, they were far from the first to launch a smartphone product. IBM's Simon Personal Communicator was first in 1994 (IBM-Simon, 2012), followed by many others, including Ericsson (R380, 2000) and Nokia (9201-Communicator, 2000). However, Apple's strategy was to focus on the user experience, bring their highly successful music player capability (iPod touch™) into the same product, and work with the Mobile Network Operators to create pull. Until then, Apple was best known for its computers and music players, and they were entering an extremely competitive market full of established and credible mobile phone vendors. Success was far from assured, but their strategic choices were sound, and their plan of action paid off handsomely, with the quality of the experience leading to significant market share within a short space of time (iphone-sales, 2018).

To understand the strategy creation process for Advanced RISC Machines, I am drawing heavily on my conversations and emails with Jamie Urquhart and Robin Saxby. Jamie was able to fill in some details from the Acorn activities and Robin from his perspective, starting from the time of his recruitment interviews for the role of Chief Executive.

Creating a strategy for success beyond the initial goals of the investors was a critical factor for Advanced RISC Machines. Without the ambitious plan that emerged, I would argue that only Apple's initial requirements may have been met. In their view, Apple had funded the venture just enough to ensure the CPU development they needed for the Newton project. In Jamie's view, Apple effectively wrote off the investment, seeing the money as an inexpensive way to develop the CPU they needed (Urquhart, 2021). Ironically, Apple's investment of approximately $3m turned eventually into $800m (Tesler, 1999). For Acorn, the story is more nuanced. They wanted the new venture to take the technology forward and develop a roadmap of higher performance CPUs for their computer products. Had ARM tried to focus on the computer systems market, they may never have succeeded in generating enough revenue to develop the roadmap longer term. As it transpired, the direction taken led to the higher performance CPUs that Acorn needed – although not before ARM had gone in directions that Acorn didn't want. More of that story in a later chapter.

Early Development of the ARM Business Plan

The journey to create the plan of action began while the technology and team were still part of Acorn, a couple of years after the launch of the Acorn Archimedes. While Acorn knew that they had great technology and a highly capable team, it wasn't obvious how they could monetise these assets. As described in the previous chapter, Acorn made several attempts to create a viable business plan for the ARM technology, with Malcolm Bird picking up the reins when he arrived as Technical Director in 1989. The business plan developed as the interest from Apple crystallised into a goal to create a joint venture. The next significant steps forward came after the agreement was signed and the recruitment of the Chief Executive began.

The Chosen Chief Executive: Robin Saxby

To help put some context around his role at ARM and impact on the initial business planning, I asked Robin about his earlier career and influences. Robin explains, "I started playing with electrical circuits at eight years old. I built stuff, particularly radio sets." After studying Electronics at Liverpool University, his first job was designing colour TV decoders. Soon Robin was approached by Motorola, looking to build their presence in the UK. He took a Sales Engineer role, where he developed solutions in a lab to get design wins. This experience introduced him to customer designs using microprocessors too. Robin believed in listening to customers' requirements and helping create solutions for them. He describes his experiences at Motorola as instrumental to his future career and outlook. The other significant influence on Robin was his time as Managing Director of European Silicon Structures' (ES2) UK company. ES2 was a start-up company focused on direct-write e-beam[15] technology for integrated circuits. Unfortunately, this endeavour didn't succeed. The market was changing quickly, the e-beam technology failed to deliver the required speed of chip

---

[15] A way to create the transistors and connections by building the circuits without having to create masks for photolithography. In theory, leading to much faster turn-around times for the manufacture of new chip designs

production, and the company was spending a lot of money, so was running out of cash. The latter was something that particularly left a mark on Robin, a situation that he didn't wish to experience again.

Robin told me of his scepticism of Cambridge companies at the time, thinking they lacked business credibility, but when he got the phone call from Heidrick & Struggles, he listened. The head-hunter explained the goal of creating a new joint venture between Apple, Acorn, and VLSI Technology. Robin knew of Acorn, having sold Motorola peripheral chips to the early CPU Limited. He was also aware of their financial struggles; however, Apple's involvement was intriguing. At ES2, Robin had seen first-hand the evolving technologies that were becoming important to the semiconductor industry, particularly the opportunity for microprocessors, semiconductor IP, and System on Chips. Robin was also President of US2, an ES2 sibling organisation based in Silicon Valley. During his time spent in the valley, he gained experience doing business in East Asia, too, particularly in Japan. He assembled a broad list of contacts across the global semiconductor industry and understood the importance of engaging with all main markets: the USA, Japan, and Europe. All of these made Robin very suited to the new opportunity. Robert Heaton (ex-Acorn VLSI lead) was now working at ES2 and told Robin the Acorn engineers were the best chip design team in the UK, and Robin was the best person to lead them (Manners, 2001).

Business Model Development

Robin told me that Malcolm shared the initial business plan for the joint venture during the interview process, and he asked what Robin thought the business model should be. The draft business plan had the idea of the ARM processor becoming a standard and licensing it to semiconductor manufacturers. However, it suggested that the new venture may also make chips. Robin thought the forecasts for Apple and Acorn chip demand were unrealistic. He was uneasy that the plan required hiring "many expensive people" and required a further funding round. Robin's starting point was to pick what he did and didn't like about the plan in dialogue with Malcolm, Jamie, and others. He didn't like the idea of making chips – feeling that they wouldn't be able to compete against the very well-funded semiconductor companies. However, work was needed to create a strategy with a financially viable plan for licensing only.

Robin was still at ES2 during this time, working out his notice but devoting as much time as he could to developing the ARM business plan and strategy. As well as drawing on input from Malcolm and Larry Tesler, he was able to use his extensive global contacts, including Cliff Roe (VP at VLSI Technology), Jonathan Brooks (future ARM CFO), and Tim O'Donnell (sales and future initial US ARM employee). Robin told me that Larry Tesler was the most help to him personally as he navigated his way forward. Soon after the foundation of ARM, Robin asked Jamie to perform a strategic analysis with the rest of the founding team. Robin wanted the whole team to be involved, not just a select few, to ensure a broad set of inputs could be heard. They carried out the Strengths, Weaknesses, Opportunities, and Threats (SWOT) analysis shown in Chapter 1.

The Initial Goals and Strategy

Although the business plan was still work in progress, there was enough clarity for the press release on the day of foundation, 27th November 1990, titled "'ADVANCED RISC MACHINES

LIMITED" LAUNCHED TO ATTACK RISC BUSINESS'. The company was to "address and attack the growing market for low-cost, low-power, high-performance 32-bit RISC chips" (Press Release, 1990).

Advanced RISC Machines Ltd.
PRESS RELEASE

"ADVANCED RISC MACHINES LIMITED" LAUNCHED TO ATTACK RISC BUSINESS

ACORN RISC CHIP DESIGNS ATTRACT U.S. INVESTMENT

November 27, 1990   A new silicon chip design company - Advanced RISC Machines ("ARM") Limited, has been formed in Cambridge, England. By exploiting the proven RISC technology designs originally developed by Acorn Computers it will address and attack the growing market for low-cost, low-power, high performance, 32-bit reduced instruction-set (RISC) computer chips.

ARM Ltd is initially backed by Acorn Computers (80% owned by Olivetti), VLSI Technology and Apple Computer. Currently ARM products are licensed by VLSI Technology and Sanyo Electric Company of Japan. The goals of the new company will be to expand the ARM technology product offerings and to promote other sources to support the expanding customer base.

The strategy of ARM Ltd is to focus on applications where ultra-low power consumption, high performance and low cost are critical. Such applications and products include personal and portable computers, telephones and embedded control uses in consumer and automotive electronics. Several of these uses already are occurring at the design-in or production stage. More than 130,000 ARM chips have been shipped to date placing it among the leading RISC processors.

more/...

Launch day Press Release 27th November 1990

The stated goals of the new company "will be to expand the ARM technology product offerings and to promote other sources to support the customer base". The strategy was "to focus on applications where ultra-low power consumption, high performance and low cost are critical". A press release is, of course, designed to create awareness and attract interest. The detail of the company's strategy for success was still far from complete.

As a statement of intent, the press release demonstrated the ambition of Advanced RISC Machines, and it's possible to get a sense of just how challenging the situation was for the company at its inception.

Firstly, the team were a relative minnow jumping into a market full of alternative microprocessor options and many competing RISC architectures. In 1990, the list of potential RISC competitors was long: SPARC, MIPS, Intel i960, IBM POWER, Motorola 88000, AT&T's Hobbit, INMOS Transputer, etc. Many of these competitors had big pockets and a growing list of customers.

Secondly, as a UK-based team, finding the "other sources to support the customer base" would require building a presence in the largest global semiconductor markets or a lot of travel for a small team.

Finally, ARM needed to build a new processor for Apple, complete contractual commitments for Acorn, and find then support new customers. ARM had a small cash runway, so they needed income quickly to achieve all three.

The strategy to achieve the goals and deal with these and many other challenges would require careful consideration.

Global RISC Standard

The directors selected Robin as the commercially focused leader needed to create a viable business plan for the new venture. He was also ambitious – Jamie told me that Robin drove alignment with the founders for much more than a lifestyle business that some may have settled for. In creating the business plan, it would need to satisfy the needs of the investors and that of Robin and the founding 12 engineers. Robin found that the directors of Advanced RISC Machines (two from Acorn, two from Apple) each had different ideas of what the business should be doing, and little attempt had been made to work out or agree on a common strategy. They each seemed to have a different agenda, and it took Robin some time to realise this and then address their concerns. He was able to use many sources of information to demonstrate that his ideas were the best way forward. For example, being part of the European Open Microprocessor Initiative (OMI) gave him much-needed information on the likely market size for licensable microprocessors.

Robin felt that the only way to satisfy all their ambitions was to make the ARM processor a global RISC standard by collaborating with semiconductor companies in all the major chip markets worldwide. The key rule was to not compete with your customers or, as Robin is widely quoted as saying for many years: "make chips over my dead body." The chosen way forward was partnership – to create long-term business relationships with silicon manufacturers and end-users for mutual benefit. It also pointed the way for the business –

ensuring the ARM processor became the global RISC standard was a tall order but was the rallying cry. It was ARM's north star goal.

"Make chips over my dead body"

Licensing and Royalties

The semiconductor companies would license ARM's microprocessor technology and pay a royalty every time they sold a chip using it. As Steve Furber had noted a few years earlier, you need a lot of volume shipments for this business model to work. Only by ensuring the ARM processor was widely used, a global standard, would there be sufficient volumes to give a good return for the company. They couldn't rely only on the computer systems markets, which were the dominant use-case for RISC processors at the time. The ARM processor needed to be a global RISC standard in embedded applications and, to achieve that, needed a market expansion strategy.

In 1991 there were very few companies selling broadly re-usable semiconductor IP – most of the semiconductor companies developed their own IP, including microprocessors, to get a competitive edge in the market. By setting up ARM as a semiconductor IP licensing company – focused on microprocessor system technology – the company would be pushing for disaggregation of the semiconductor IP itself. ARM would design the base technology and deliver embeddable macrocells to semiconductor companies. Those companies would then integrate the processor with their proprietary technologies to generate any SoC device they desired.

Why would they invest in ARM's microprocessor rather than use their own? The answer lay in return on investment – it was challenging to achieve sufficient chip sales to pay for developing proprietary microprocessors. By licensing from ARM, as well as gaining access to a state-of-the-art, low-power RISC processor, they would all benefit from sharing key software components and development tools for this processor. Licensing from an independent company like ARM was also preferable to using a competitor's microprocessor technology.

Transistor scaling ensured there were growing business opportunities for microprocessor-enabled SoCs. Many semiconductor companies had already started to build CPUs. For those companies, Not-Invented-Here (NIH) would make it challenging for them to buy ARM's CPU IP later. However, the costs required to develop and maintain a CPU and all the necessary additional components were already starting to increase rapidly. They were also finding out how difficult it was to establish new CPUs in the market. The software to support these systems was becoming a more prominent component of an end system's functionality, and the cost of software development was rapidly increasing. ARM's strategy was to target embedded applications with more complex software requirements than traditional 8-bit processor systems, where the total development costs favoured using a standard microprocessor.

ARM was founded right at the beginning of the industry's System on Chip revolution. Although US company

MIPS[16] sold their R2000 microprocessor as a standalone chip, by 1988, it sold the R3000 as an embedded microcell (R3000, 1988). The move to 32-bit CPUs had significantly increased the costs associated with microprocessor development – offering a CPU for a license fee that had known capabilities was a genuinely innovative step forward for the industry. ARM chose to differentiate itself from the company MIPS by not allowing customers to change the design: "ARM users wanted an ARM to be an ARM", whoever was the manufacturer (Urquhart, 2021). This was a deliberate strategy to cement the ARM CPU as an industry standard with known hardware and software interfaces, making it more attractive to the OEMs.

It is tempting to assume that the licence plus royalty business model would benefit ARM's finances only. However, I believe the model benefitted the industry, too. That might seem counterintuitive. How would semiconductor companies, OEMs, and the industry benefit from a royalty model? The answer lies in the balance provided in the financial transaction and the timing of the payments. If sufficient companies licensed a product, the licensing fees could be set attractively for each, thus lowering the barrier for new companies to invest in the 32-bit RISC processor IP. By collecting the licence fees upfront, ARM was able to fund the current business while the royalty payments were far from guaranteed and far into the future. The team built the business plan assuming the company could break even without royalties in the near term.

---

[16] Originally an acronym for Microprocessor without Interlocked Pipelined Stages but confusingly the same as the popular measure of CPU performance: Millions of Instructions Per Second (MIPS)

The genius behind the licensing plus royalty business model was that it significantly motivated ARM to help the semiconductor companies get their chip designs into volume production, not just to prototypes. Robin encouraged ARM to consider the semiconductor companies as partners, not just customers, working with them for long-term mutual benefit. Then ARM treated the OEMs as the real customers, understanding their needs to create pull from them to the silicon partners (SiPs). ARM would be rewarded financially only when the SiPs were rewarded financially by selling to the OEMs, and the royalties were low enough that the SiPs earned an order of magnitude more return than ARM. A genuinely win-win business model – possibly the most innovative thing ARM ever did. Compared to developing and maintaining a bespoke microprocessor family, a licensed microprocessor core is more cost-effective and lower risk, even when considering royalties.

The Advanced RISC Machines 1991 Business Plan

By August 1991, the first complete business plan crystalised and articulated aspects of the fundamental business model and strategy critical to later success. It had taken Robin this time to get all the Holdings board directors to accept that the partnership model proposed was the right one for the company. The critical elements of the ARM plan were now clear:

- The ARM CPU was to be open to all, and the company wished to remain independent of the semiconductor companies and OEMs. ARM was also part of the European Commission's Open Microprocessor Initiative (Commission, 1990), having transferred membership in the research project from Acorn.

- ARM would license its technology to a wide variety of semiconductor companies, "each with different strengths", with royalties as the bonus for volume manufacture.

- The semiconductor companies and other third-party collaborators were described as "partners". Long term relationships for shared success were vital.

- ARM would target partners in each major geographic area: Europe, the USA, and East Asia. New licensees should increase market share, not just be second sources.

- The ARM CPUs would be an industry standard with no modifications. An "ARM is an ARM" whichever manufacturer used the IP.

- ARM CPUs were positioned as the leading RISC embedded controllers, targeting a wide variety of markets, including "battery-powered, portable products", "imaging products", and "mobile telecommunication products", to name only three.

- The emphasised technical benefits of the ARM CPU changed the game versus competitors:

- Reduced system cost by using RISC techniques to deliver CISC-like performance at significantly lower costs

- Best Performance efficiency: Millions of Instructions Per Second (MIPS) per $

- Best power efficiency: MIPS per Watt

Other elements of ARM's operational strategy were not written in this plan but confirmed by Robin and Jamie. Some of these were associated with the culture, which I'll explore in the next chapter. For example, the 1991 business plan was created as a prospectus to attract new investors to improve the business's independence. However, Robin wanted to reach profitability without resorting to further investment, so he was focused on start-up survival, minimising unnecessary expenses, and getting purchase orders for anything possible (Saxby, 2021). They were determined to grow behind revenue rather than eat into their financial reserves.

Another key element emphasised by Jamie was that the plan was always under discussion and highly evolving. The action planning was almost continuous – something that was very much part of the culture while I was at the company, too.

Hindsight tells us that this early plan and business model largely worked, but when Advanced RISC Machines set out, little of this was validated or certain. They wanted it to be true, but many business models can look good on paper. Only long-term success can validate them. The first steps were to validate that licensing the technology was possible to additional semiconductor companies in the target regions. If they couldn't sell any licences, then either the technology, the business model, or both might be wanting.

Strategy Validation

The goal was to license the ARM CPU in all three major regions, the USA, Europe, and East Asia. Their founding licensee was US-based, VLSI Technology, so their attention turned initially to the other two.

As Sales Manager of the time, Jamie told me how he got in touch with many European Semiconductor companies, but

GEC-Plessey Semiconductors were the only ones who showed an active interest. This was incredibly convenient as they were UK-based, making the travel and communication considerably more straightforward, and Robin already had an established relationship with their Managing Director, Doug Dunn. They were looking to add a CPU to the building blocks they could offer customers but were very cautious. After much deliberation, many meetings, and building a test chip, they agreed to purchase an ARM licence.

This licence agreement was an exceedingly important milestone in the young company's journey. Founding employee Dave Howard told me of his memories of Robin waving the payment cheque around the office to celebrate closing this first deal at the end of 1991 (Howard, 2021). It was a proof of concept for the model; however, GPS were a relatively minor player in the worldwide semiconductor market. It gave the business another six months of financial runway, so it was vital. The goal had been to debug the process of selling this licence model – ARM was determined not to be a UK-centric or even Europe-centric technology provider but had to start somewhere. They had also learnt some crucial lessons in the process, including the importance of building both technical and financial advocates (known internally as disciples) within the prospective partner.

Emboldened by this success, the senior team continued to target Japan, including Sharp, who was to manufacture the Apple Newton MessagePad™. ARM leveraged the Apple relationship, got Sharp excited that Nintendo might also benefit, and enlisted help from Sharp's US and European offices. This deal was not easy, but after a year and monthly visits by Robin and others, Sharp signed the licence in mid-1992 (Urquhart,

2021). The many trips to Japan had also led to investment interest which Robin was holding in reserve. With a dozen or more potential licensees, ARM was determined to raise its profile in Japan. ARM simultaneously announced the Sharp licence deal, the appointment of the first Japanese employee, Takeo Ishikawa, and investment by Nippon Investment and Finance Co. Ltd. (NIF) of ¥100m.

The next licensee was a surprise for ARM and a good one. Following a presentation by Mike Muller[17] at the Microprocessor Forum in December 1992, Peter Rheineke, a technical fellow at Texas Instruments (TI), became an evangelist for this very elegant, low power 32-bit processor. TI was a pioneer in the semiconductor industry, having produced the first commercial silicon transistor and invented the integrated circuit in the 1950s. It was a significant player in the industry whose well-oiled machine knew what it wanted. The contract negotiations were very challenging, with ARM having to significantly improve the detail of deliverables and contractual obligations. This corporate learning benefitted ARM enormously in later partnership deals. The deal was finally signed in mid-1993, with ARM's business model having been tested robustly and found to be sound. Despite the differences in commercial power, ARM maintained its non-exclusive licensing business model while TI gained the assurances it needed for future commercial success and access to the technology.

The TI deal had significantly boosted ARM's credibility. The business model now looked well-validated: new licensees in

---

[17] Head of Marketing at this time, later CTO for many years

Europe, Japan, and the USA, with licence fees paid early and royalties paid on later chip sales.

Partner Reactions

Not everybody was comfortable with the TI licence. The first manufacturer of Acorn's ARM microprocessor and co-investor, VLSI Technology, was very unhappy. Not only was TI a powerful competitor, but it was also in a legal dispute with VLSI Technology. A great deal of communication was necessary to smooth this over – this type of reaction was common while the number of partners was still relatively small. However, ARM's strategy would have needed a lot of change if existing partners could influence the choice of future partners. The strategy was to maintain independence and openly license the CPU technology to partners who could offer new market opportunities. Robin says that he initially turned some partners down as they just wanted to act as a second source supplier for existing opportunities. For example, it was only when LSI Logic (a US semiconductor company) said they would use the ARM processor to target the disk drive market that ARM agreed to license them. More partners in different markets encouraged more support from third-party providers of tools, software libraries, and operating systems. Thus, lowering costs and barriers for all partners and making the ARM processor more attractive to OEMs. Gradually, the early licensees were more accepting of ARM's free choice and the benefit of expanding the market opportunities and ecosystem support.

The CPU licensing business progressed slowly at first. Cirrus Logic added to the TI licence in 1993 and two more in 1994, with Samsung Semiconductors being highly significant in the longer term. With the announcement of the ARM7TDMI®

CPU in 1995, the number of new partners grew by five each of the years 1995 to 1998. Momentum was firmly established for the business model.

Another welcome benefit of the partnership model was that some partners would recommend individuals for ARM to hire if, for example, they had microprocessor design skills. Skills that the partner preferred to have inside ARM than elsewhere.

Strategy Evolution

By 1993, the big chunks of the strategy were now in place, with strategy validation well underway. However, it is very rare for a plan of action to survive 'contact with the enemy'. It was no different for ARM. Review and adjustment were necessary in the light of new or improved information. Jamie explained that the work on strategy was deeply rooted in the current context and was always very consultative and nearly continuous. One such example was the decision to invest more in consulting services, and another was in software development tools.

Consulting Services

ARM had provided consulting services for Acorn Computers as part of its founding commitments, building the floating-point design, FPA10[18] and the SoC, ARM250[19]. Later, Acorn contracted ARM for the project I first worked on in 1993: the ARM7500™[20]. The FPA10 chip development in 1991/2 had

---

[18] Floating Point Accelerator – a plug-in accelerator on Acorn's RISC-PC computers

[19] Used in the Acorn A30x0 and A4000 computers of 1992

[20] Used in the Acorn A7000 computer of 1995

used more resources than hoped, with almost no long-term gain (Acorn sold only around 500 of these accelerators). The ARM250 and ARM7500, on the other hand, were System on Chip developments combining many existing elements using relatively small teams. Not only did these projects take few or no processor designer heads, but the chips also had the potential to enable new customer applications. If ARM was to do any consulting, this type of development seemed to point the way.

By 1994, despite the previous year's launch of the Apple Newton MessagePad and an increasing number of other design-ins for the ARM processor, it was clear that the time to meaningful royalty revenue was going to be much longer than envisioned. After IP delivery, the road to volume chip production was slow and challenging, with many projects falling by the wayside. The industry still had too few engineers who had experience integrating processors of any type, and ARM's deliverables needed to mature. If ARM was going to grow, it would need to help smooth the road to volumes.

There was an opportunity to expand ARM's consultancy business beyond Acorn and make a little bit of money along the way. Warren East, a future CEO, was recruited to lead the consultancy operations – with the primary goal of helping the partnership build chips around the ARM IP. ARM needed more design-ins, an accelerated time to royalty, and to enable our partners' success.

This evolved element to ARM's strategy yielded notable early successes, such as the ARM7100™ SoC in 1996 that became the very low power device at the heart of a new PDA: the Psion Series 5. The full significance of this became clear later with the creation of the Symbian software joint venture, a spin-off from Psion's development (See Chapter Seven – Ecosystems). The consulting business also hastened ARM's relationship with some new semiconductor partners, improved ARM's on-chip bus standard, Arm® AMBA®, accelerated ARM's software developments, and eventually led to Systems IP and Software Systems businesses.

Development Systems

A CPU's value in a system is its enormous flexibility of function – driven by the software it runs. Acorn, and then ARM, had been acutely aware of the necessity and importance of providing support tools for system developers: compilers, assemblers, linkers, and run-time libraries. A third of the founding team were specialists in these areas, and a growing list of partners demanded more capability. Acorn's release of Acorn RISC Machine development platforms had enabled third parties to develop software development tools, too. ARM had choices to make regarding this provision for the partnership. One option would have been to deliver bare-bones tools solutions and rely primarily on third-party tools developers for the community. Instead, by 1996, ARM chose to invest more fully in producing and selling development systems products for the partnership. The 'DevSys' business emerged with a clear mandate: to always be the first to support the ARM processors' capabilities, offer excellent hardware and software tools, and enable third-party tools vendors. Like the consultancy business, the DevSys business was created primarily to support and accelerate the design-in of ARM processors but was tasked with pulling in revenue to cover their development costs and, if possible, help bridge the gap to future royalties.

Strategic Revision and Extension

That initial action plan proved a solid foundation, validating the fundamental premise of offering licensed RISC processor technology with royalties. Depending on your viewpoint, luck or good marketing led a TI technical leader to spot and then champion the ARM processor, leading to possibly the most impactful licence deal in ARM's early history. However, as Chapter Six, "Admit when you're wrong", explains, ARM had to overcome some serious obstacles to realise its dream of targeting deeply embedded applications. And when ARM better understood the reality of the timeframe between licensing and royalty flows, new action plans had to be created to enable and accelerate design-in activity.

With Robin's leadership and a talented team, by the end of 1997, Advanced RISC Machines had built a company with revenue of $44m, a net profit of over $8m, just over 274 staff (ARM, Annual Report, 1997), and a lot of market momentum. The total invested capital had only been approximately $4m, and Advanced RISC Machines had been cash generative and profitable every year from 1993 onwards. With the Initial Public share Offering (IPO) of April 1998, the newly renamed ARM Holdings plc now had to live up to the expectations of a much broader set of investors.

The initial strategy had been built, tested, and evolved. Now a more thorough review was required to build on the core business and take the company to another level. Time for the first significant strategy revisit.

1998 – 10x03

In the first of many major strategy reviews and revisions, ARM embarked on the project "10x03" – ten times revenue by 2003.

The goal was to energise the organisation and set a tone: "You may think we've been successful, but there's so much more to do." This exercise involved a broad cross-section of staff across the regions to ensure it was as inclusive as possible. The most notable new action that emerged was the need to increase ARM's software resources significantly and target more software-derived revenue. As well as maintaining momentum in the existing processor licensing business, the review also highlighted the many untapped areas of licensing opportunity ahead. Another action to emerge from this process was to split the market into eight segments, with the goal to have ARM technology in everything digital by 2010. The tagline *The Architecture for the Digital World*™ was born and used for 15 or more years. The process also gave ARM confidence that it could continue with a very high growth rate.

2002/3 – ADAPT

With 420m ARM-based chips shipped in 2001 and over 75% share of the mobile phone market, it is reasonable to say that the ARM microprocessor had been established as the global RISC standard for embedded applications. ARM had arrived. But now it had a problem.

Mike Inglis joined the board team as Head of Marketing in 2002, bringing a wealth of semiconductor, commercial, and business consulting experience. On a tour of the sales teams, he remembers the European Sales Lead asking him, "What am I going to sell next? I've sold everything!" (Inglis, 2021). ARM needed some new product directions and challenges.

Fortunately, that year ARM had already embarked on its next strategic planning process, called ADAPT. This process built upon the learnings from 10x03 and had five primary objectives:

1. Create a plan to achieve a fourfold increase in revenue by 2006

2. Create a plan to achieve >35% market share in all eight market segments by 2006

3. Develop a new list of business ideas to build on current strong market positions

4. Develop a diverse 'idea development' pipeline to fuel growth beyond 2006

5. Gain a greater understanding of ARM's competitive position

In keeping with ARM's cultural norms, the process objectives were:

– to be as inclusive as possible

– to be a global plan where each region contributes

– to have a review process to make progress visible

– to have a communication process to share the output

By July 2002, the main conclusions were presented to the ARM Holdings board. There were a lot of ideas, some of which would bolster existing product types, some for new product types, and some for dealing with emerging industry threats and opportunities.

Unfortunately, that quarter, ARM was severely distracted. In 2001, the semiconductor industry suffered a catastrophic 32% reduction in sales relative to the boom year of 2000.

The downturn was partly a hangover from the "irrational exuberance"[21] of the dot-com bubble. Fortunately, ARM's business had plenty of momentum and had been growing strongly, but by the 3rd quarter of 2002, the weakness in the semiconductor industry caught up with us. Our licensing revenues took a big hit relative to our expectations, necessitating a reduction in headcount with all the pain that involves. The 4th quarter was one for keeping the business stable and preventing any further revenue drops.

Despite this setback, for the entire year of 2002, ARM's revenue was marginally higher versus 2001, at $214m with a $73m net profit (ARM, Annual Report, 2002). The processor licensing business had grown strongly to over $117m, and the partners shipped 456m ARM-based chips.

In the 4th quarter of 2002, Mike Inglis picked up the ADAPT output to re-establish momentum and led ARM's executive team through weekly strategy meetings. This resurrected planning exercise delivered a set of well-defined strategic directions in the first half of 2003, building on the hard work of ADAPT.

Among the many areas that ARM chose to invest in were microcontrollers, higher-performance CPUs, security extensions, data processing engines, graphics processors, system-level design tools, and physical IP. This was a smorgasbord of opportunity which would represent the first significant broadening of the company's product portfolio since

---

[21] 1996 speech by the then Federal Board Chairman, Alan Greenspan

its founding, marking a significant shift away from purely being a CPU licensing company.

"Preserve the Core/Stimulate Progress"

The strategic revisions continued beyond ADAPT, with the next major update in the 2008 timeframe spurred by the rapidly evolving smartphone and tablet markets. And early in the following decade, Arm started serious endeavours to create a new business to supplement the core IP licensing business. By 2013 Arm had identified an IoT (Internet of Things) focused business as the most likely way forward. In 2014 Arm was restructured into the IP Products business and a separate (and somewhat protected) IoT Services business, starting with the Arm® Mbed™ OS for IoT.

In the book *Built to Last*, there is a chapter called "Preserve the Core/Stimulate Progress" (Collins & Porras, 2004). Arm is notable for just how successful the core processor licensing business has been from that early validation in the 1990s to the time of writing this book. That continued success owes a lot to the desire to drive the business to achieve more. With the benefit of hindsight, it's clear to see the enormous impact of revisiting the strategy in small evolutionary steps with occasional significant leaps, then driving those action plans hard.

Such is the nature of the industry that some challenging goals have taken many years to result in meaningful market share – both short-term and long-term planning was necessary. For example, in 2003, the strategic goal was to win significant volume in the microcontroller sector. Accounting for the time to design the IP, then license it to many semiconductor partners and for them to build many products, it was not until 2011 that volumes of the Arm Cortex®-M family processors exceeded 1 billion per year. The momentum behind the strategy led to over 10 billion per year by 2017 – a figure which continues to grow faster than any other sector.

Another lesson from Arm is that by keeping activities aligned to the core business, as Arm has pushed into new areas, it also had the pleasing side-effect of driving the core business. What seems clear in hindsight is that every time Arm invested in a new but related product range, it was also increasing the competitive position of the core CPU technology. Expanding into physical IP helped Arm grow the business through that business's revenue, and it also helped demonstrate better performance and power consumption for the processors. And Arm's actions to strengthen the product capabilities and ecosystem to support the partnership in the face of the Intel x86 assault into mobile (see Chapter Nine) paid off through increased interest in Arm's processor technology.

When Things Don't Work

Unless you're incredibly fortunate, not every strategic plan will work as expected. Markets may develop unexpectedly, competitors may react aggressively to counter your moves, or the execution may not meet your expectations. Of course, not every action plan Arm embarked upon led where we hoped. Many succeeded, but only partially; some beyond our hopes, but a few withered and died.

Learning from these scenarios is what matters most for an organisation. Arm's open and non-blame culture gave us a great platform to assess results objectively. For the most part, the failures and nearly-but-not-quites led to better, more appropriate plans. An example may help.

Arm's early plan to build a dedicated Digital Signal Processor (the Piccolo project) met with intense opposition from some partners and didn't offer the financial opportunities we hoped. We followed up by adding DSP instructions to the CPU architectures and focused on software library development instead. A later attempt to build a related data engine business led to an acquisition and the OptimoDE™ product. That product didn't succeed directly, but Arm created AudioDE™ with the technology which provided ultra-long battery life for millions of portable audio players.

Chapter Summary and Lessons

With a cycle of approximately every five years, there was a major review, then expansion and evolution of the action plans. In all these different strategy planning exercises, one thing stayed constant: the need to validate, review, and revise continuously. Arm's industry environment is dynamic, full of opportunities and threats – only by creating bold plans, then trying them out, listening and modifying was Arm able to successfully surf the waves of growth.

I believe Arm's experiences highlight some essential lessons:

1. **Technology and People Foundation**. The technology was excellent, but it wasn't in a 'me-too' category. There was a uniqueness to combining RISC-like performance with low system cost and power efficiency. This uniqueness enabled Arm to target new product categories and markets. The people chosen to be

founders of Advanced RISC Machines were extremely talented, experienced, and capable of driving the selected action plans at pace.

2. **Filling skill gaps**. Robin Saxby was recruited as Chief Executive to bring his strong commercial experience to the business. He, in turn, brought in the necessary Finance, Legal, and Sales resources to ensure a balanced team.

3. **Challenging but Collaborative**. Robin immediately challenged critical elements of the strawman business plan for the start-up – not accepting what he was given as written in stone. He used his network and the existing resources to collaboratively create a plan that he believed would satisfy both the investors' requirements and the ambitions of himself and the team.

4. **Resources and Partnership**. When Robin looked at the business plans for the potential joint venture, he realised that they would need to work with the prominent semiconductor vendors if Arm's meagre resources were to have maximum impact. The licensing and royalty model was chosen with the clear choice to not compete with customers by staying out of chip manufacture. Arm chose to focus on partnerships with semiconductor companies, end-users, and third parties.

5. **Put a stake in the ground, and move towards it, learning as you go**. Although the strategy creation and evolution process was nearly continuous and highly collaborative, Arm always established a clear view of the long-term and intermediate goals. By heading in a direction, review of progress and modification was

possible. The alternative would have been paralysis by analysis.

6. **Aim high but start small**. The plan was to create a global RISC standard, which meant licensing many semiconductor vendors globally and achieving a leading market share. However, with limited resources and an unvalidated business plan, ARM had to start somewhere – the deliberate culture was to experiment cheaply and quickly. By engaging a local semiconductor vendor (GPS), ARM validated key elements of the licensing plan with limited risks and costs. The next step was to secure a significant vendor in Japan, which was much more difficult but would bring more substantial marketing benefits.

7. **Be real**. One thing that consistently characterised Arm's business planning was a ruthless focus on reality. By ensuring we had representatives in all the key markets and an open, communicative, and trusting environment – Arm gave itself the best opportunity to understand the harsh reality of what its customers saw and needed. Strategy development was always rooted in the reality of resources, technology, opportunities, and threats.

A topic conspicuous by its absence in this chapter is that of the creation and nurture of Arm's culture. The culture underpinned the strategy creation process and execution considerably, so this is the next chapter's topic.

Three: Create and Sustain the Right Culture

Peter Drucker is famously credited with the saying, "Culture eats strategy for breakfast". This saying does not mean that strategy is unimportant, but rather that a strong culture will generally make or break a company's best-laid plans. The culture was one of the most impactful elements of Arm's success, and it was intertwined with the business and partnership model. To understand the positive influence of Arm's culture, we will explore the predominant culture found in the Cambridge office in the early years, the one I'm most familiar with, and one that had the most impact early on. This culture was an amalgam of inherited culture from Acorn Computers, the joint venture's founding culture, and successive waves of new employees, all working towards Arm's common goals.

In the book *Built to Last*, there is a chapter called "Cult-like Cultures" (Collins & Porras, 2004) – there are elements of a cult-like feeling to the culture that grew in Arm. We used to talk about people being Arm-shaped. In a conversation, we might say: "Carol is very Arm-shaped" or "that wasn't very Arm-shaped behaviour", but what did we mean by that? We didn't have anything written down to say what it meant in the early years, but we all had a sense of its key components. If someone was collaborative, constructive and understood the bigger picture of what Arm needed to achieve, then we might say they had "it". If they tended to work for their own benefit, only cared about their local goals, or didn't collaborate openly, we wouldn't consider them Arm-shaped. Like the 'cult-like' examples from *Built to Last*, there were some people who just couldn't fit in. They weren't able to operate in our environment and needed to move on.

What were the origins of this culture, and why was it an essential contributor to Arm's culture and success?

There were cultural foundations on which the founding 12 and Robin Saxby, the first CEO, could build. The new company's culture, though, was deliberately created in conjunction with the strategy through consultation and debate (Urquhart, 2021). They wanted to ensure they started with the right set of behaviours that gave them the best chance of succeeding.

Let's start by exploring the culture inherited on the day of foundation, then exploring some of the key elements they wished to promote, and finally, how the culture was embedded and evolved as Arm developed.

Inheritance

The Founding Twelve

Two of the first employees of what was to become Acorn Computers, Steve Furber and Sophie Wilson, were a powerful influence on those that later founded ARM.

Dissatisfaction. Steve recalls Sophie telling him, "I can do better than that," when she first saw his MK14 system built for the one-armed bandit (CACM, 2011). Later, after the release of the Acorn Atom, their dissatisfaction led them to design a computer with better expandability, which became the BBC Microcomputer. And in 1983, when they had eliminated all the reasonable options available, they decided the only way forward was to build a microprocessor based on RISC principles but applied in a unique and power-efficient manner. Their desire for elegant technology solutions had led them to continuously challenge the existing options, even when they had been part of their creation. They had a never-satisfied culture, always aiming higher.

Can-do Attitude. The story of building a demonstrator for the BBC (Wilson, 2012) illustrates another aspect of that team's behaviour: a can-do attitude. One of the best illustrations of this you could ask for was designing and building a new computer system from ideas on scraps of paper in four-and-a-half days. They knew the task was unlikely to succeed, but they went for it anyway. A team with many different skills, pulled together, determined to make it work, with the exceedingly trusting and supportive encouragement of Hermann Hauser, did the near impossible.

Trust and Empowerment. Sophie gives credit to Hermann and the other technically competent managers who trusted them to do the right thing, so when they said they could build a new microprocessor from scratch, they were believed. Hermann continuously looked outwards to understand the broader context and encouraged the team to do the same. Seeing the developments in the RISC concepts, for example, and encouraging the team to look in that direction.

Shared responsibility. Designing computer systems and silicon chips is a team effort, and intense cooperation is needed to be successful – there are so many complexities and things that can go wrong. The rudimentary tools available in the 1980s, combined with the leading-edge designs embarked upon by Acorn, meant that they needed to create their own tools and processes to have confidence in the result. Manufacturing a prototype silicon chip was relatively expensive and time-consuming, even then. The methods put in place by the system and VLSI engineers included the block specification reviews (described in more detail in Chapter Five). This methodology was highly impactful for several reasons: it encouraged a very open and honest feedback mechanism of each other's work; it enabled engineers to learn from those more experienced colleagues; it improved the quality of the designs; and, perhaps most importantly, it encouraged a collective responsibility for the results. If a mistake was made, which was inevitable in any complex activity, there was a shared responsibility without blame.

World-class, talented, computer system design knowledge. By the time of the agreement to create the joint venture, the 12 engineers had been working with each other for some time, creating complete computer systems and multiple chip designs. They had experience cooperating, learning from each other, and being technically successful. The first year of ARM doubled down on these traits, as they worked extremely hard to deliver to both Acorn and Apple's requirements with too few resources. The team had a strong self-efficacy - a belief in their ability – and it helped that they were each very talented engineers.

Technology Passion. Thinking of the many attempts to find a way to save the ARM technology, it's clear the founders were very motivated to make the new business work. They wanted the technology to be used and proliferated – they were incredibly proud of what had been created (Urquhart, 2021). This feeling of pride and passion helps frame why the team was so keen to show Apple how good they and the technology were during Apple's initial fact-finding visit. It also frames many early partner and customer meetings, with all ARM employees being strong advocates of the technology and its potential.

Initially, however, they were missing the commercial experience that Robin was able to bring.

The New Chief Executive

Of course, Robin's prior experiences were essentially why he was selected to lead Advanced RISC Machines. He also brought a set of cultural attitudes that complemented those of the ex-Acorn engineers very well.

Commercially focused business leader. Robin's early sales engineering roles, through to his business leadership roles at ES2, ensured he was highly focused on customer requirements and the need to build a solid profit-making business. The experience of seeing ES2 run out of money had a strong impact, too, and he told me of his determination to manage ARM's cash: get a purchase order for everything possible and spend money very wisely.

Collaborative, Open, and Global Mindset. Robin was naturally collaborative and open, preferring dialogue and discussion with many voices to resolve complex challenges. He was also very well connected across the industry and regions, so he came with a global mindset: I often heard Robin say, "Think global, act local."

Deliberate Design of ARM's Culture

The new company's challenge was not building the technical competence needed. It was creating an organisation with strong commercial behaviours. Whereas Acorn was, for the most part, a Business to Consumer organisation (B2C), Advanced RISC Machines needed to be a Business to Business (B2B) organisation, selling technology directly to other technology companies. That and ARM's modest resources would mean bringing greater commercial awareness to the whole team. Robin was selected as the CEO for his commercial experience, but he was offered the job before meeting the Acorn engineers. He needed to ensure the 12 engineers would accept him as their leader. They were a tight-knit team with years of experience working together. He was a commercially focused outsider, and not from the Cambridge area.

Jamie Urquhart recalls that after the joint venture was agreed upon, he and Tudor Brown were taking Larry Tesler of Apple back to Heathrow on one occasion, so they agreed to meet Robin there (Urquhart, 2021). The meeting was enough of a success to suggest a further meeting with the rest of the team. They arranged this meeting at the Rose and Crown pub in the small village of Ashwell, about 25 miles drive from the Acorn office. This location was apparently chosen to be mid-way between Robin's home area of Maidenhead and theirs of Cambridge – actually, it's much closer to Cambridge. Despite this, Robin arrived first, and things didn't start on the best foot. The Acorn team misjudged how long it would take to get to the pub on a cold and foggy November evening. They arrived after Robin, and, as John Biggs describes it, Robin greeted them with, "You're four minutes late – another minute, and I'd have gone!" (Biggs, 2021). Fortunately, things improved significantly from there. Robin asked the team whether they wanted him as their leader, and they said, "Yes." The 12 engineers certainly knew they were dealing with a leader willing to speak his mind. Robin had taken along Brian O'Connell, ES2's UK Director of Engineering, whom he wanted to meet the Acorn engineers and trusted his opinion. Afterwards, Brian must have given Robin a positive account of the Acorn engineers.

Robin wanted the team to accept him as their leader, but he also wanted to work in collaboration to harness all of their skills and knowledge. Jamie explained that as well as discussing and debating various business plan elements, they also deliberately chose the culture they needed to support the plan. The strategy and the culture were co-designed, with one supporting the other. These things didn't arrive overnight but through dialogue and debate, with many late evening meals among the leadership team. What emerged formed a solid foundation for the business.

"Brutal" Honesty

The new employees of Advanced RISC Machines faced enormous challenges, although they knew they had excellent technology. The team already had a very strong working relationship and could be open and honest with one another. Robin's arrival was a spur for change, but if they had not included Robin in their working culture of openness, the enterprise could have been stalled at birth. Instead, Jamie said there was an agreement to be totally honest with each other so that no information was hidden – Robin used the term "brutal" honesty (Saxby, 2021). They deliberately chose the culture of openness that they wanted to create and maintain. In this way, it was possible for the team's first SWOT to fully identify their weaknesses and threats. So armed, a better business planning process was possible. For example, the honest recognition that they had no patents helped drive them to develop new ideas and products which could be patented. That attention to patenting ARM's inventions would, more than once, benefit the company significantly over the years to come.

Lean and Mean

Advanced RISC Machines' founding investment was sufficient to fund the team for perhaps 18 months only. The new company had to find a way to satisfy its investors' requirements, which would mean new product development and additional team members. Robin was determined that the company should stand on its own two feet as soon as possible, avoiding the need to ask investors for any new money (Saxby, 2021). He emphasized getting purchase orders for everything possible to help instil a strong commercial focus in a team previously at arm's length from paying customers.

Robin also wanted them to remain "lean and mean". Two stories illustrate the mindset of the new organisation, both driven by Robin's determination not to repeat his ES2 experience of running out of money before winning sufficient business.

On the day of foundation, the team were still in-situ in the Cambridge Water Works building that Acorn occupied off Fulbourn Road, Cambridge. They needed to find their own office space quickly. Robin tells the story that one option Acorn had identified was a new office block north of Cambridge at Vision Park, Histon (Saxby, 2021). Robin didn't want to waste their initial investment funds on "fancy new offices", and soon, they found a converted turkey barn on a farm in Swaffham Bulbeck – just north of Cambridge. This office was lower cost, had character, and got people out of Cambridge (albeit only a few miles).

'The Barn', Swaffham Bulbeck, Cambridgeshire, UK

When they had visitors from abroad, it helped them stand out as something unique and showed they were ploughing their money into the technology, not office buildings.

As well as stopping the new company from renting plush new office suites, Robin didn't want to hire "expensive VPs" where he didn't need to, either. Before foundation, Jamie describes how Robin met three of them in a pub, The Chequers in Cherry Hinton. Robin asked Mike Muller to be Marketing Manager, Tudor to be Engineering Manager and, much to his surprise, Jamie to be Sales Manager. It was a shrewd use of their respective talents. It would be quicker and lower cost than training up new external people and would prove crucial to the company's future development.

Inclusive and Collaborative

Jamie described the working culture of the founding 12 as being like a rugby[22] team where it didn't matter who scored; it was about the teamwork that got you there. They had a lot of trust in each other and had been "cast out" from Acorn together. Dave Howard describes how on hearing about the plan for the new venture in mid-1990, he thought its chances of success were low but felt it was better to stay together as a team (Howard, 2021). Once away from Acorn, Dave remembers they were determined to find ways to make money, and Robin's commercial experience and drive couldn't come soon enough.

Fortunately, Robin's perspective was well-matched – he described a training course at Motorola on synergy, which notably demonstrated the importance of teamwork and the power of inclusiveness. He wanted to create this kind of culture and worked to ensure many voices were heard in discussions and debates. As the existing team wanted an open and collaborative environment, an inclusive leadership style would inevitably sit well with them. This behaviour was one of the foundations of being ARM-shaped.

Flat Hierarchy

This related cultural assumption had its roots in the founding team, too. John described the feeling of 'no hierarchy' as one of the cultural elements that helped make a big difference. Although there were reporting lines, there wasn't a feeling of distance between the managers and the team members. John

---

[22] Pick a sport you're familiar with where the team is more important than any one individual. For the British, rugby is viewed in this manner

recalls that Mike and Tudor were particularly rebellious against management and hierarchy (Biggs, 2021). Their attitude was that everyone should feel equally able to contribute and debate, regardless of who was involved. This was probably highly significant to the ongoing cultural development as the company grew, especially as Mike led the Marketing activity and Tudor led Engineering during those first few years.

With a flat hierarchy came an expectation that managers would not micromanage their teams. The management role was to support the highly capable, although potentially less experienced, team members. If employees had felt the hierarchy too strongly, they might have tended to always look up for instructions rather than sideways for guidance.

Keep Getting Better

I will return to this theme in Chapter Five, "Build a Delivery Machine", as a strong driver to improve ARM's project delivery. Jamie told me that he viewed 'keep getting better' as a designed cultural statement, along with 'build something, then build it much better'. As a young organisation with an emerging business strategy and a fast-changing industry, they needed to acknowledge the impossibility of getting everything right the first time. During those early years, I heard Robin say, "Try a bit, learn a bit," to encourage that attitude in us all.

Partner/Customer Focus

There is no doubt that the team understood the importance of customers – their very existence was closely tied to delivering the technology required by Apple for the Newton project and finding new sources of revenue to survive as a company in the short term. Robin brought not just commercial experience and drive but also a list of global contacts in the industry. He was a natural networker, and Jamie saw this rub off onto the rest of them. Being Cambridge, UK-based, it was inevitable that some founders would soon become accustomed to a lot of travel for customer meetings. Winning the first licensee, GPS, involved a lot of meetings, albeit within the UK; winning their first Japanese licensee, Sharp, resulted from 12 months of frequent visits to Japan by Robin, Mike, Jamie, and others.

Partnership. The chosen business model came with the strong desire to work with the semiconductor companies for long-term mutual benefit. Hence their agreed cultural norm was to call these companies ARM's "partners", not customers. Of course, they were paying ARM directly, but the point was to set the culture to view them as partners, something explored further in Chapter Seven, "Build an Ecosystem of Shared Success".

Building Rapport. The style of engagement with partners was also notable, with Robin illustrating the importance of building rapport with people. Robin wanted the partner to feel good about working with ARM – he wanted them to come back for more. John Biggs tells this story as a great example of Robin's style. When, in early 1991, they needed to fill the barn with office furniture, a salesman visited wanting to sell oak-veneered workstation desks, as the photos would look good in his company brochure. Robin sensed a negotiating opportunity, telling the salesman he just wanted plain desks. After agreeing to supply oak-veneered ones at the same cost as plain desks, Robin tried to get a custom-made desk for the boardroom for free. After some time, to settle the discussion on the boardroom table that day, Robin suggested they toss a coin – the salesman lost, and ARM got the boardroom table for free. Then on a roll, Robin took him to the Black Horse Inn down the road, where they chatted, and he challenged the salesman to a game of bar billiards for desk drawers. This time, Robin lost, so the team never had desk drawers in the barn! (Biggs, 2021) The story illustrates what Robin did well: he established excellent relationships with people. Even when negotiating hard, he tried to make people feel good about the deal – he was always looking to the longer-term relationship and partnership. These rapport-building skills helped win over early customers with ARM's openness, honesty, and intent to partner.

Embedding the Culture

With Robin and the 12 engineers came the inherited and foundational culture driven by the challenges ahead. As new employees arrived with greater frequency, the essential aspects of the desired culture needed to be embedded in the growing organisation. The culture would be very dependent on the actions and behaviours of the existing employees. Whether they realised it or not, they were the role models that people like me watched and followed. Fortunately, the deliberate culture of openness, flat hierarchy, and a high-trust environment created the right environment to embed these attributes into the organisation – a virtuous circle.

Openness and Collaboration

One of the defining hallmarks of the ARM environment, a collaborative culture, was shaped by what ARM was trying to achieve. The rugby team mentality of the founding group extended as more people joined. When I joined in mid-1993, there were around 35 people in the barn, and the sense I had was of joining a very friendly and helpful group of people. There was a spirit of openness and collaboration, which resonated with my preferred working style. The impression was of a well-bonded team that welcomed new members with open arms – "please come and join us on this quest".

The licensing and royalty business model backed that quest, "To be the global RISC standard". The business model also demanded that ARM extend the openness and collaboration model into the partnership. ARM's resources were tiny compared to the semiconductor companies and other industry players. Success was only possible if the partners were selling ARM-based chips in volume. It drove us to want to partner with customers and third parties – whatever it took to help get ARM's processors designed into chips and sold in large numbers. We believed it was to our mutual benefit to work collaboratively and openly with our partners. And that behaviour was an extension of how we worked with each other internally. All parts of the organisation needed to deliver for ARM to best achieve our goals. Being ARM-shaped meant you understood this and worked to ensure our mutual success.

Hard Work and Fun

It was a phrase used regularly in the early phases of Advanced RISC Machines. It was born out of, on the one hand, the need to ensure the success of the small enterprise through sheer hard work; and, on the other hand, a desire to enjoy the journey along the way. It may have taken dozens of trips to Japan to win the Sharp license deal in 1992, but it was important to savour the moment and acknowledge the vital milestone towards the bigger goal.

The hard work was necessary to ensure the engineering team delivered the working chips to both Acorn and Apple; and that the commercial team found new customers and new sources of income. If either had failed, then the company's fate would have been very different. ARM immediately put new joiners into high-expectation projects – I, for example, joined a team of two building the ARM7500™ SoC for Acorn with challenging timescales.

We were also introduced to all our new colleagues and, where possible, given the opportunity to socialise outside of work, too. My timing was fortuitous, as, at the end of my first week, there was an event held on the River Cam – yearly in those days: The Cambridge Computer Company Charity Punt Race. We arrived to see most of the company directors already wearing their Advanced RISC Machines T-shirts, ready to get very wet. The punting was at a minimum; we propelled the punt upriver with any possible device to Grantchester meadows, where food was served and prizes handed out. We were immediately welcomed into the family.

Punting by Grantchester Meadows in circa 1995

There were also pub lunches at the local village pub, The Black Horse Inn, but one of the surprising company traditions was the VLSI group lunchtime walks. Harry Oldham (VLSI group leader after Jamie Urquhart had moved to sales) loved walking. So most lunchtimes, the VLSI team and anyone else interested would go for a 30-minute walk from the barn into the Cambridgeshire countryside. Quaint, unexpected, and surprisingly valuable. Friendships were formed quickly and easily that remain to this day. Those friendships were part of creating a collaborative working environment for delivering projects with challenging technology in very tight timescales. Any disagreements could quickly be resolved in front of a whiteboard with openness, honesty, and speed. Those VLSI lunchtime walks were a surprisingly effective way to improve our innovation and productivity. There's something about walking and talking side-by-side that promotes openness and honesty.

There were summer BBQs, Christmas parties, and "payday pigouts" – designed to welcome the rapidly growing teams to the organisation. The work was challenging, and very long hours were required on occasion, but the goal was to ensure we stayed as a team united in our quest and enjoyed the successes along the way.

"Hard work and fun"

Conferences

ARM ran a lot of internal conferences. The early ones were an excuse to get everybody together, called Global Operations Conferences (GOCs), and as ARM grew, they became more focused. Nonetheless, they acted as a powerful way to keep us informed, embed the culture, and, most importantly, renew or make new relationships with people across the business. These conferences gave the opportunity to spread the cultural expectations of openness, honesty, and determination to succeed.

Inevitably, as ARM grew, it wasn't practical to continue these in the same form – the GOCs evolved into much more focused introductory events for those new to the business, called "The Big Picture". They are run in different regions on a regular timetable, with all new joiners invited to attend one in the first six months. Senior and experienced ARM people present information about how the business works, with group activities to get people mixing and working together. The most significant benefit of these events is the relationships forged between people from different groups and geographies. Despite its growing size, these diverse and sometimes long-distance relationships help act as a glue for the organisation. And possibly most importantly, install the feeling that everyone is part of the same company working together, albeit on different aspects, to achieve the common goals.

Evolution and Growth

A few months before the IPO of April 1998, Advanced RISC Machines was 274 employees strong at the year-end. It was a decent, small to medium-sized company where it was just possible for senior people, like Robin or Tudor, to have had some interaction with everyone in the company. All the leadership team operated an open-door policy, with an expectation that conversations could happen between any level of the organisation. The culture and behaviours of the organisation had become very firmly embedded. However, as the company grew further, some of the behaviours expected would need to evolve, and more effort was required to spread them to the growing number of new employees worldwide.

Jamie explained that he believed the culture could not remain rigid but had to evolve, especially as ARM hired into new offices outside the UK. However, there were elements of the culture that needed to be kept similar across borders for ARM to perform at its best.

Core Values

With continued expansion and increasing numbers of non-Cambridge and non-UK employees, ARM needed to articulate the concept of what we felt it meant to be ARM-shaped. ARM needed to set expectations among the current colleagues and new joiners wherever they were located. In the year 2000, the employee count exceeded 600 for the first time. It was now impossible for the personal interactions between board members or senior managers with others to be sufficient to spread the cultural norms. Bill Parsons joined in early 2000 as EVP of Human Resources, and he facilitated an exercise to extract from the leadership team what behaviours or core values really mattered – ARM was no longer a start-up. They honed down these core values into four:

- **Constructive Proactivity** – don't wait for instructions, do what is right for the company

- **Selflessness** – work for the organisation, not yourself

- **Customer and Partner Focused** – create what our partners need

- **Responsiveness** – keep the pace high, don't block partners or colleagues through inaction

These did not imply that some behaviours were no longer necessary, just that their relative importance had reduced. For example, as a colleague of the barn era, I felt the spirit of 'lean and mean' very strongly and held onto that sense of frugality for years after it was no longer critical to success. Likewise, 'work hard and have fun' was much more of the site by site or project by project mantra. When there are 400 people to cater for, it's hard to organise cakes for the Cambridge office on your birthday.

Measuring Behaviour

For ARM, it wasn't enough to declare that the Core Values were the behaviours expected by delivering some company presentations and putting them in the company 'handbook' – ARM took a game-changing additional step which ensured they became embedded into our world. When it came to performance reviews, everyone was judged both on delivery and the behaviours related to the core values. 50% was for delivery against expectations (What), and 50% was for behaviour against the core values (How). Therefore, the overall rating explicitly favoured people whose behaviour was ARM-shaped, and they delivered. This rule was transformational both as an individual and as a manager, allowing helpful conversations with colleagues regarding how things should be done. It also allowed managers to address the issue of high performers who didn't work collaboratively with others – such people were no longer able to hide behind their ability to "deliver what was asked" without dealing with the collateral damage of their behaviours and relationships.

Professionalisation

There's no doubting the professionalism of colleagues at ARM – they were and are a highly talented group of people. What I mean by professionalisation here is associated with the company as a whole – let me explain. ARM was, from its foundation, a company dominated by engineers. Even with over 5,000 employees, around two-thirds come from an engineering background. Back to the beginning, when Robin selected Mike to be Marketing Manager and Jamie to be Sales Manager, they both had been active engineers. Engineers and ex-engineers permeated the culture of ARM. To some, this may sound like nirvana; to others, a dystopia. Engineers have a wonderful (or annoying) habit of believing that they can solve any and every problem with enough analysis. Engineering is inherently a creative endeavour, always striving for better ways of doing things, and debating with an expert in a field outside engineering is just sport for an engineer. This behaviour, however, can be very disempowering for those joining an organisation from a different profession.

While Robin took care to build the skills of the initial 12, he also understood the need for professional expertise where needed. He brought in David MacKay as ARM's lawyer, part-time initially. Peng Wong was initially loaned from ES2 to deal with the finances, and Robin brought in Wilf Marshall as a consultant on strategy and people development. As ARM grew, so did the number of non-engineering specialists required to help deliver the company goals: lawyers, accountants, marketing communication specialists, human resource specialists, etc. The culture needed to evolve to truly embrace these additional professionals within the business. ARM was no longer all about engineering. At the 2015 ARM Leadership Conference, the issue was brought to a head, and a small team catalysed the creation of a successful 'Project EveryOne' initiative.

Cultivation and Adaption

Maintaining the most effective culture for an organisation can be likened to gardening. There may be an initial deliberate design, although it will inherit the nature of the location, for example, dry and sunny or damp and shady. The intentional design needs to take the current resources into account and build on them, or get radical and dig areas up and start again! Once the initial desired design has been established, the garden needs cultivating – just as the desired culture will need to be kept alive. In some areas, the 'right' plants will have thrived and can be encouraged. In others, the 'wrong' plants will need to be moved elsewhere or removed completely.

To stretch the analogy, if an opportunity arises to extend the garden (build a new business), great care will be needed to ensure the plant choices for that area will be appropriate and can thrive. A new business with different customers may need a different ethos to drive success. However, it was important for ARM to maintain a common thread of culture through the various businesses. The organisation was chasing the same big company goals, i.e., increasing the number of ARM-based royalty-bearing chips sold and increasing the total value of the IP, and hence royalty, on each chip.

The cultivation of culture needed to allow different variations in different areas while holding onto a core, hence the core values. ARM also needed to adapt as the organisation grew and evolved.

Innovation

With this diversity of profession and business functions came an increasing expectation of collaboration across disciplines and operations optimisation.

Innovation in new product development comes almost for free in an engineering organisation. While Advanced RISC Machines was founded with precisely zero patents inherited from Acorn (who had none to give), the company was soon able to start creating its own distinct sets of patents. The early SWOT identified this lack of patents, so ARM made plans to ensure the new technology developed incorporated patents wherever possible. Every product on the roadmap would create challenges in the hunt for better performance or power consumption. Put such a challenge in front of skilled engineering teams, and they will soon find inventive ways to overcome them. Innovation was a deliberately chosen cultural value right from the beginning.

With a larger company, the desire for improvements to operational efficiency and effectiveness soon leads to the need for innovation to be encouraged across all departments and activities. And so, Innovation was added as a Core Value – ARM was making it clear: being innovative in whatever work you do was essential and a cultural value. It was also important to not allow the drive for efficiency and effectiveness to hold back product innovation. Organisations can indeed become more risk-averse; ARM's inoculation was the constant pressure from its partners to bring new technologies and features to market in a highly competitive environment.

Personal Development

In a company with high growth rates, where the board of directors collectively know every individual by name, personal sponsorship of individuals into new roles is relatively easy and effective. Robin believed in building the team's strength and wanted to ensure developmental training and opportunities were available from very early on. Under Wilf Marshall's direction, opportunities for learning beyond your current role were offered; for example, many of us enjoyed SPIN® sales training (Rackham, 1995) – another effort to build a commercial understanding among the pre-dominantly engineering staff.

ARM continued to provide plenty of growth and development opportunities; however, it became necessary for individuals to take more responsibility for their development and growth. There comes a time when you won't be automatically known as someone with ambition and potential by senior managers in the organisation. And so, Personal Development was added to the Core Values at the same time as Innovation. ARM was making it clear that ownership of your development was expected – you can't rely on the organisation to do all of this for you. The Learning and Development team can provide a wealth of training courses, but it is up to the individual to work with their manager to plan their own development and advancement.

Core Beliefs

Around 15 years after the initial capture of those core values, as a multi-thousand-person company, the essence of what it meant to be Arm-shaped was re-evaluated and simplified into three core beliefs (Arm-code-of-conduct, 2021).

These three beliefs were curated by working groups and managed to encapsulate what many of us have felt for a long time – the essence of being Arm-shaped. They represent a logical evolution of how the company expressed what the culture of Arm should be. When very small, everyone had an implicit view of what was needed from each other – role modelling and peer pressure did what was required to spread culture. As the organisation grew beyond the visibility of the directors, capturing the essence of the behaviours most valued resulted in the original Core Values, which were then extended even further with additional growth. And finally, when the danger was of extending the Core Values too far, the next logical step was to simplify down to the essence of what's important:

We, not I – Work for the organisation, not yourself. Collaborate and partner.

Be your Brilliant Self: Bring your best self to work, apply your skills and knowledge for the good of all – it's good to have a different view.

Passion for Progress: Innovate; Develop; Solve problems; Be responsive; Get things done.

Words of Warning

Negative Outliers

There is now more recognition in business journals that encouraging the positive aspects of the required culture is possibly less than half of what's needed. For many organisations, the lived culture will evolve towards the worst that is tolerated. Suppose one department's team leader is allowed to focus on their own needs, excluding collaboration with other departments. In this situation, it becomes increasingly hard to expect inter-department collaboration. This behaviour is sour milk in your coffee – it's impossible to ignore, however good the coffee.

What allowed ARM's culture to remain strong and healthy in most places, most of the time, was the intolerance of negative behaviours – ARM had a low tolerance for negative outliers. Differences were tolerated and celebrated where possible, but negative behaviours were not. ARM people expected that anyone who wasn't able or didn't want to play the ARM-shaped game was dealt with by their manager or department. There was no hiding when it came to review time and peer pressure.

Cultural Challenges

Although the book focuses mainly on the positive aspects of ARM's culture and actions, it is worth pointing out a few downsides of the strong culture. Firstly, it could never truly be universal. All sufficiently large companies will have too many different personalities and local cultures. Related to this fact, it's true to say that ARM's early culture was born out of a predominantly British set of norms. These ways could easily jar with other cultures; for example, the British tendency to downplay and look for areas of weakness versus the US tendency for optimism and looking for strengths. Overall, I believe we managed these cultural differences acceptably through shared purpose and regular interactions. Other areas of the culture, though, had some downsides which were not nation-based.

The can-do culture sometimes led to less experienced colleagues failing to speak up when they believed something wasn't possible. The sense of 'we have to be able to do this' overrides the 'total honesty' of what the challenges really are. This danger makes it even more crucial that leaders and managers take the time to listen to concerns and create an environment where trying hard and failing is acceptable – as long as lessons are learnt. The other challenge of the can-do attitude is that in many places, ARM built a hero-culture of individuals getting things done despite the tools available. This hard work and determination to overcome barriers were vital for growing the operational machine at one level. However, people move on to other roles, and the company scales too far for the 'hacks' to continue working. The Organisational Development Conference of 2012 had a significant thread on 'Organisational Scalability'. There was a corporate acknowledgement that ARM needed to build systems that no longer depended on individual 'heroes' holding them together.

Chapter Summary and Lessons

In 2012, Google set up Project Aristotle to answer the question: "What makes teams effective at Google?" (Google, 2016). After four years, they concluded it was less about who was on the team but more about how the team worked together – paraphrased by some headlines as "just be nice to each other" (Independent, 2016). Many of the founders of Advanced RISC Machines were indeed very nice people who were friendly and helpful. However, they were more than that; they also valued total honesty about the current situation and healthy disagreements, searching for the best way forward. They didn't want the management hierarchy to get in the way of progress and encouraged a 'flat' organisation. The organisational culture that hundreds of us experienced was one where you were free to speak your mind without fear of repercussions. This feeling is now called Psychological Safety and was found to be the most important factor for Google. Teams that had Psychological Safety, that were able to disagree and discuss openly and constructively, were more likely to succeed than those that didn't. Arm had this and more.

Culture for Arm was and always will be a massive factor in its success. It greases the wheels of progress and makes it a great place to work. What lessons can we draw?

1. **Perform a Culture Audit** – Take note of the culture you're inheriting among the people you've got, the good and the bad. What do you want to keep, and what do you need to lose?

2. **Design the Culture you Need** – Determine the culture you need for success, and supplement from the top-down. The engineers from Acorn had a great

working relationship and a can-do attitude but needed the new CEO, Robin, to show them the way with customer engagement and business drive. To fit the chosen strategy, some cultural statements were then agreed upon through dialogue and debate.

3. **People are Watching and Listening** – The culture will be role modelled by people in positions of power and influence – the 'Leadership shadow'. Ensure they are suitable role models for the organisation, and be aware that people will copy what they see and hear. Having agreed on the required culture, it needs to be the everyday style among the leaders and influencers.

4. **Give Equal Value to Behaviour and Delivery** – and embed them in the performance review system. Ensure there is nowhere to hide for either managers or individuals. Culture needs embedding and retelling regularly.

5. **Culture Needs Cultivating** – just like strategy, it requires building, reviewing, and evolving… again and again.

6. **Be on Guard for Misalignment** – The culture tolerated by managers is the culture you will evolve towards. Deal with the negative outliers and fast – give people the support needed to help them behave or help them out the door. The example set by the action of dealing with the "sour milk in the coffee" will be as important as removing the disruption itself.

Four: Get the Customer's Voice Inside

Stating the obvious, the goal of Arm is long-term sustainably growing revenue and profit to reward its investors. Things were more nuanced initially, with technology development being the primary aim of the two leading investors, Apple and Acorn. However, the leadership teams' ambition was to see the technology used as widely as possible (the global RISC standard). Achieving this would generate revenue to invest in future development and reward the investors (employees were shareholders, too).

ARM's chosen business model was to generate revenue from four primary areas: technology licensing, royalties, software tools, and services. Consider a hypothetical perfect scenario: ARM would develop only one of each product type (starting with the CPU) and license each to every semiconductor company, which OEMs would use in every market application with 100% share. Likewise, ARM would sell the software tools to every possible end-user. This hypothetical (and unrealistic) scenario maximises revenue and minimises development costs. The realistic goal would be to have as few products as possible for as many markets as possible.

The point of this thought process is to help explain many of the decisions behind ARM's strategy and organisational design.

By understanding all the potential markets, ARM would be able to design its products to be the best fit for all these applications. Working with OEMs would ensure their particular needs, such as their preferred silicon suppliers, were understood and addressed. Working with the silicon partners would ensure the product could be integrated smoothly into their design flows and give them the deliverables and training needed.

So, ARM needed mechanisms to bring this knowledge into the organisation at many different levels. Jamie Urquhart reminded me of the term "Cambridge black hole thinking" when encouraging colleagues to look outside and think about ARM's partners. The long-term success of ARM owes a great deal to just how well the voice of the customer was embedded inside the organisation. The way the culture was directed, the way ARM was organised and operated, all intertwined to create an organisation uniquely tuned to sensing and responding to the needs of semiconductor partners, the OEMs, and the industry trends in general.

Some Challenges

ARM's goal was to have all the information and knowledge needed to achieve the best outcome and to have an organisation sensitised and reactive to this information. What were some of the particular challenges faced by ARM?

A Meagre Set of Resources

The founding group of 12 engineers plus a CEO did not make a large set of resources. If ARM were to spend its development resources wisely, it would need to harness its partners' and customers' combined resources. With a wealth of markets that the ARM processor might be suitable for, it was necessary to partner with the licensees so that their greater marketing resources could work for ARM's benefit.

The Technology is Complex

Designing and building a leading-edge microprocessor requires specialist talent and experience. However, the interface between the processor and the rest of the system was where partners had their specialist knowledge. It was imperative ARM found ways to engage partners in their domain – to learn and then design better products. As an R&D led company, ARM would live or die by its ability to solve complex problems for partners and customers.

The Rate of Change of the Technology and Markets

Since the birth of the integrated circuit in the 1960s, the number of transistors that can be manufactured reliably on a single chip has grown exponentially. This rapid growth has led to a breath-taking rate of change in the semiconductor industry and the markets that use that technology. The average mobile phone has the power and performance of a laptop computer from barely a few years ago. However clever ARM's employees might be, they will never be able to stay on top of all the possible trends and changes in the market. The best ARM can do is have a lot of sources and do a lot of listening.

Being UK Founded

Being a UK-based computer company probably played against Acorn's worldwide recognition and sales ambitions – the dominant computer markets at the time were in the USA and

Japan. Acorn computers were neither the low-cost games computers like the Commodore Amiga nor seen as business machines like the IBM PC and the later clones. The UK home and education markets were just too small to give the revenues needed for Acorn.

For Advanced RISC Machines, being UK founded was the spur needed to play globally from the start. Robin Saxby and the founding team were determined not to repeat the previous outcomes and needed to ensure that the UK designed technology would be successful in the high-volume markets wherever they might be. ARM's success may have possibly[23] been assisted by being seen as neutral and non-competitive to both the US and Japanese semiconductor vendors of the day.

Advanced RISC Machines' founding direction was driven by many interlinked factors, partly explaining how the customer's voice was and is so strong within the organisation.

Partnership and Shared Success

The consequences of choosing the technology licensing model were profound, impacting just about every business element, from the organisational structure and internal culture to how ARM worked with partners, customers, and third parties. For example, the semiconductor vendors were described as partners, not customers. Robin believed strongly in creating long-term relationships of mutual benefit and wanted ARM to be at the heart of a partnership of companies – each contributing their

---

[23] Just my opinion, but lightly held

unique capabilities, leading to the promotion of the ARM architecture.

During my time at the company, I rarely heard the word "customer" used. By default, we automatically talked about "our partners". The change of terminology may seem trivial, but it was highly effective. As ARM colleagues, we were continually reminded by the partnership terminology that ARM was seeking a mutually beneficial relationship with customers and key suppliers. And organisations interacting with ARM would hear themselves described as partners or potential partners. There could be no doubt of the desire to form a longer-term relationship.

The requirement for long-term relationships is also driven by the response time of royalty revenue to ARM's efforts. The time from initial customer interactions to license agreement, to working silicon, to volume manufacture, could be anywhere from 12 months (in exceptional circumstances) to 5+ years. During that time, ARM needs to provide support for the partners while continuing to sell licences, services, and tools to pay the bills. ARM was set up as a company with long-term payoffs and needed a long-term relationship with its partners. That extended to key suppliers and third parties, too.

ARM, therefore, aggressively pursued a partnership strategy from the beginning; not just an aggressive strategy to win customers but also an aggressive strategy to partner with the industry. If the industry were successful in using ARM technology, then so would ARM be. This model may seem a grandiose notion for such a small company, but CPU technology has a large footprint within the semiconductor industry. The choice of a microprocessor will impact many significant aspects of the SoC design and software development activities. The software footprint may be extensive, too, extending to the customers of the SoC vendor, the OEMs, and a whole ecosystem of third-party developers, e.g., the App stores for Apple and Android phones.

Cultural Impact

Therefore, using the terminology of 'partner' was appropriate and important to sensitise ARM's colleagues to the impact of their actions. There was a culture of trying to do the right thing for the partner, whatever was written in the contract, to ensure that a partner could be successful. When mistakes or misunderstandings occurred, we always tried to admit them and fix the problems as quickly as possible. The long-term relationship and the promise of future royalties were the keys to this behaviour.

To keep us aligned on the key company goals, at some point in the 90s, Robin had set a challenge of achieving 100 million ARM-powered chips shipped in the year 2000 – something that felt like a pipedream in 1997 with only 9.8m chips shipped (ARM, Annual Report, 1997).

The partnership culture drove a 'jam tomorrow' attitude to royalty revenue. ARM fought hard to drive revenues in the short-term to keep us growing and sought to remove the barriers to volume shipments. Fortunately, with some very significant design wins in emerging volume markets, most notably digital mobile phones, ARM's partners experienced exponential growth with volumes of over 350 million by the year 2000 (ARM, Annual Report, 2000). The 'unrealistic' target of 100 million was significantly exceeded, and royalty revenues became meaningful at around 25% of the $150m revenues for the year.

I remember the general feeling was of never quite believing the units shipped and royalties would grow that fast, keeping us keenly focused on driving partner licensing and design-ins.

Geographic Presence

The early action plan to validate the business model was to win licensees in Europe, Japan, and the US, so getting feet on the ground in each region was imperative. Jamie explained that while ARM was a British technology company staffed initially in the UK only, the leadership team didn't want to export Britishness (Urquhart, 2021). They wanted to understand the market and customer needs from colleagues on the ground in the key geographic locations.

The first concrete step forward came in July 1991 with the appointment of Tim O'Donnell in the heart of Silicon Valley in California. Tim had been a colleague of Robin's in the US sibling of his previous company, ES2, and according to Robin (Saxby, 2021), Tim implored him for a role within Advanced RISC Machines. However, Robin didn't have enough money to employ him full-time, so they agreed to pay him as a 50% part-timer – shared with his then-employer. Tim soon joked with Robin that he seemed to be working full-time for ARM but on half-pay! Tim was able to stay close to Apple, the reason for ARM's existence, keep up with the news coming from Silicon Valley, and introduce ARM to key opportunities while spreading the word.

In 1990, Japan was the second-largest semiconductor market and was a more challenging proposition, with a powerful semiconductor industry and a more Japan-focused approach. Breaking into that market would be challenging, with language and cultural barriers to overcome. ARM started with a press tour accompanying VLSI Technology and then used a local company to arrange a seminar to highlight the ARM technologies. The first opportunity chased successfully was Sharp Electronics Corporation, which had been selected to manufacture the Newton MessagePad product for Apple. Without an ARM presence on the ground, the team made many, many visits to Sharp and other prospects over 12 months. Robin was then introduced to Takeo Ishikawa by a contact at VLSI Technology, and in early 1993, Ishikawa-san became the first employee in Japan. Like Tim, in the US, his role was to keep close to the key customers and communicate the market needs and opportunities back to the still primarily Cambridge-based team.

In the years leading to the IPO of 1998, the focus on those two markets initially helped ARM win nine additional US-based licensees and nine additional Japanese licensees. Targeting these key market leaders with local leaders had paid off handsomely. In addition, four licensees were added from Europe, serviced initially from the UK; however, two others came as a welcome surprise.

After the Texas Instruments licence deal of 1993, Jamie received a phone call from a representative of Samsung Semiconductors – Samsung also wanted a licence. At that time, early in its global journey, Samsung wanted to emulate what the best of the others were doing and were very aggressive. After only four meetings, in May 1994, ARM announced Samsung as their first partner outside the big three regions, and the following year LG Semiconductor also became a partner. Following the successful strategy of hiring someone with deep local knowledge, Sam Kim soon became the country leader for ARM Korea.

Over time, regional leaders for Taiwan, China, Israel, and continental Europe followed – in each case, they became integrated members of the ARM leadership team, coming to internal conferences and communicating regularly to ensure their partners' voices were heard.

Marketing R&D

In 1991, with the engineering development teams working on the floating-point accelerator, FPA10 for Acorn and the ARM6 developments for Apple, additional resources were needed for very close technical engagement with prospects. As Acorn had found with their manufacturing partner VLSI Technology, good knowledge of processor systems and software was required to help customers evaluate and design a CPU into their SoC. VLSI Technology had often called upon Acorn staff such as Jamie to help at specific opportunities. Now, ARM needed to simplify and accelerate the evaluations and developments of ARM technology. Dave Jaggar and then Dave Flynn were recruited in 1991, forming a small team under Mike Muller, Head of Marketing.

Dave Flynn told me (Flynn, 2021) that Mike wanted 'Marketing R&D': working with potential customers at a very low level, most often helping with software evaluations of the ARM CPU. They created the very simple Platform Independent Evaluation (PIE) board to enable porting customer software for evaluation. And the more sophisticated Platform Independent Development (PID) board to showcase the chips from VLSI Technology and other licensees as chips became available.

The two Daves worked closely with licensees and prospective end-customers and were instrumental in demonstrating the benefits of the RISC technology in some embedded applications. However, they also were learning some of the limitations which were holding design-wins back. In particular, the size of the software code for a 32-bit RISC processor could be much more than CISC based or 16-bit alternative processors. More of this is in Chapter Six.

By working very closely with potential users, they were able to accelerate decisions to invest in an ARM licence, learn a lot about the practical application of the technology in customers' situations and, most importantly, bring that knowledge back into the heart of the company.

Lead Partners

One of the critical goals of the global licensing strategy was to harness the semiconductor partners' more significant resources and market knowledge. ARM wanted to design the IP that its partners needed to succeed and grew a very strong culture of working with lead partners while developing new processor IP. ARM's selfish goal was to learn from that partner to ensure the processor IP was very well suited to the target applications and that multiple other partners would also want to license the same product. The ideal situation would be to have an OEM and a semiconductor partner work with ARM to ensure the specification was correct and that the application's speed, area, and power consumption were ideal. The partners would essentially be leading ARM into a new application space. They would benefit by having a considerable influence over ARM's design decisions and have a temporal advantage over competitors in the market.

In this way, ARM was able to de-risk product development, having a high likelihood that we would find additional licensees to share the development costs of the IP and that future royalties would accrue. The methodology also had the direct benefit of connecting the engineering development team directly to a partner, pulling strongly for the project to be completed. A person's willingness to spend discretionary time and energy on a project is much greater when they feel this direct connection.

For some applications, there were only a small number of potential licensees. However, for the mobile market in the 2000s, we might often find several partners wanting to become lead partners. In such cases, ARM had to take care not to overload the system – too many partners might make it too difficult to deliver in a timely and effective manner. The number of lead partners was also a good indication of the likelihood of success of a product commercially and the potential delivery challenges. Zero lead partners indicated that the IP development was probably unsuitable for the market – great feedback. Only one lead partner led to the danger of bending too far in their direction and not making the IP sufficiently flexible to be of value to others. Between two and four lead partners were probably ideal, with the ability of the team to give each enough attention and some assurance the product would be suitable for the intended market application.

Working with lead partners evolved and enabled some very significant steps forward – two examples below illustrate. I could have described dozens of others.

Apple and the ARM610/ARM710

Apple had initially invested to ensure very close control of the direction of the ARM developments. Their focus was to produce a new class of product, the PDA, for which they needed a CPU with good performance yet within strict power and area budgets. The ARM6[24] core was the first new CPU design completed by Advanced RISC Machines, with Apple giving a lot of guidance into what they needed versus the existing Acorn-designed processors. VLSI Technology, GPS, and Sharp were the first licensees of ARM610, hoping to supply Apple with the SoCs they needed for the Apple Newton MessagePad product, while also searching for other applications. Apple led ARM towards more flexibility with a full 32-bit address bus and support for a broader range of operating systems[25]. ARM later updated the design, creating the ARM710™, which Cirrus Logic licensed in 1993 and also wanted to supply Apple and target audio markets. The ARM710 and its variants were used in many other SoCs by partners. So, the original development led to multiple licensees and design-ins, all following the direction guided by Apple.

NEC, ARM11MPCore and Automotive

In 2004, after delivering the first ARM11™ products, a debate was raging in the industry about the best way to add performance to CPUs. Was it best to build bigger, faster single CPUs? Or add the ability to interleave multiple software threads on a single processor core (MIPS Inc's multi-threaded approach)? Or would a multi-processor (MP) with shared memory be the best

---

[24] ARM's previous core was the ARM3 – Larry Tesler suggested ARM leapfrog to ARM6 as Intel had released the 80486 in 1989 and Motorola the 68040 in 1990

[25] The ARM Holdings board had immediately come to show its value as Acorn were unhappy that the ARM6 would require them to rewrite key parts of their software and so weren't supportive

approach? ARM's analysis pointed towards multi-processor being the most flexible, scalable, and power-efficient way forward, but it would require a lot of investment to find out. Enter NEC of Japan, a partner since 1995 but had previously used MIPS CPUs for their high-end products. They, too, wanted to build a multi-processor solution and were willing to partner with ARM to make it happen. Their focus was the development of high-performance CPUs for automotive Infotainment systems. In 2005 ARM was able to release the ARM11MPCore™ CPU with the ability to run software on up to 4 separate cores, all sharing a coherent view of memory. It was a hit with other partners, too, looking for scalable performance, and MP capability became the standard solution for all subsequent Application class cores, starting with the Cortex®-A9™ of 2007. Multi-processing technology was one of ARM's most significant steps forward and came when we were in intense competition with MIPS in non-mobile applications. It nearly didn't happen, though, with the initial MP research happening in ARM's Sophia Antipolis office despite a top-team request to cut the activity from the budget to balance the books. By the time of Cortex-A9™ and beyond, the technology was necessary for ARM's battle with Intel's x86 in mobile.

In each example, the partner acted as a lead, introducing ARM to a market opportunity and helping us understand those applications' specific requirements. It was a crucial element, helping to ensure ARM's processors became the most widely shipped 32-bit processors in history.

Consulting Services

As described in Chapter Two, ARM decided to invest more resources into providing consultancy services in 1994, with

Warren East initially leading the activity. By engaging with customers on SoC designs directly, ARM was soon to discover just how much it had to learn.

Many of the early users of the ARM IP were sophisticated chip designers who could work with the early deliverables, however basic. Using ARM IP was a bit of a black art, involving semi-custom implementation techniques and many manual verification steps. So it was easier for many new partners to ask ARM to do the SoC integration. ARM would need partners to build the SoC designs themselves to accelerate royalty revenues. Before that could happen, ARM needed to engage, learn, and evolve its offerings.

By engaging with partners directly, we were able to bring knowledge of the challenges of SoC design straight into the business. A much wider group of engineers saw first-hand the areas where the ARM technology excelled and where it needed to improve. This "eating our own dog food" was particularly championed by John Biggs (Biggs, 2021) – it was essential for us to understand what ARM's partners found when using ARM IP. ARM also experienced using the EDA tools from the perspective of the SoC designer with the CPU as a black box to be integrated. This and many other insights enabled ARM to evolve the design methodologies and IP deliverables.

Sales

It's an old adage that "People buy from people", but this may seem irrelevant and terribly old-fashioned in the era of internet shopping – however, context matters. Arm's context is a B2B business producing leading-edge IP and tools. Any sufficiently complex or new technology will not be purchased at the click of a button on an internet shopping site. The licensee will often design their system simultaneously with Arm's design of the new IP. Or they may not have used Arm technology before and need detailed technical meetings to ensure they are using it most effectively. The relationship between the people in the semiconductor partner and Arm is crucial. For new IP, it is not a transactional experience for either side.

For this reason, Arm soon employed Partner support engineers dedicated to major partners, which later led to Partner Managers. Their role is to help the partner maximise their return on investment in Arm technology. They network within the partner organisation and Arm so that the people with the required knowledge and expertise can be brought together whenever needed. An Arm Partner Manager once drew a diagram for me: a tree of branches on the left-hand side coming down to a single stem through the middle; and a similar but different branching structure on the right. His role in the middle was to find the right people in both organisations and connect them when needed to ensure success. Those people could be architects, hardware or software engineers, lawyers, licensing or finance people – anyone required to ensure success at different stages, from early discussions through contract negotiations, to IP and Tools delivery and use.

"Partner Managers, not Sales Managers"

A Partner Manager succeeds when their business partner succeeds. The partner should come back for more IP, more development tools, and ship more royalty-bearing silicon if we are successful together. And it provides a rich vein of information flowing from the partner into Arm, ensuring high-quality feedback from specialist to specialist on everything from architectural design features to legal terms in a contract.

Segment Marketing

Robin told me how his time at Motorola significantly impacted his understanding of markets and growth. When he came to ARM, he realised that there was an opportunity to make the ARM CPU a global standard for use across multiple markets. The idea of market segments was key to ensuring the small company didn't put all its eggs into one basket, whether desktop computing (Acorn) or handheld devices (Apple). The strategy was to have partners operating worldwide, each focusing on different markets.

Initially, ARM was primarily reliant on the information gleaned from the relatively small number of partners themselves. With increasing licensing success, ARM added specialist resources to directly understand the requirements of different market segments. ARM wants to be able to plan a roadmap of products well suited to the market needs – to an extent to get ahead of some of the partners. The challenge for the product development teams is to hear the market input and translate that into the best possible IP designs. By understanding the market segments more thoroughly, the strategy is to design products suitable to cover as many potential applications as possible while maintaining their performance, power, and area advantages.

This scenario first came to fruition with the synthesisable ARM9E-S™ CPU core of 1999, which was used to create a family: ARM966E-S™, ARM946E-S™, and ARM926EJ-S™. The ARM966E-S was suitable for real-time applications such as disk-drive controllers; the ARM946E-S targeted a new generation of inkjet printers and baseband controllers; the ARM926EJ-S was used to run the user-facing operating system of mobile phones and PDAs. All sharing components and architecture as far as possible.

A better understanding of the different market segments helps Arm build other IPs to suit various applications, for example, Arm® Mali™ Graphics Processing Units (GPUs) and, more recently, Arm® Ethos™ Machine Learning Inference engines.

Ultimately, the main impact of good segment marketing information is helping Arm to prioritise between different IP development options. Over time, Arm has produced a wider variety of products suited to a more extensive set of applications. By understanding the market size of each segment, Arm also helps the partners grow at the highest possible rate.

Keeping Technical Leads Connected to the Customer

A common organisational challenge is keeping key technical developers connected to the customer as an organisation grows. Mathematically, the surface area to volume ratio reduces as the volume increases: it becomes harder for the voice of the customer to make it through the layers of sales and marketing to the engineers developing the products. Arm is no different from any other here; the danger grew quickly. The main line of defence employed is to use Product Marketing specialists whose role is to work with the technical leads on the one hand and the partnership on the other. Arm also wants the technical leads to be brought into partner meetings as soon as possible. The technical leads need to be able to explain the technology, receive feedback directly, and establish a relationship with the technical leadership within the lead partners. Connecting technical leads reduces the danger of messages being lost in translation or simply being dismissed as too difficult to achieve. If the technical lead hears for themselves the partner's "unreasonable" requirements, they are more likely to be able to arrive at compromise solutions that will work across the partnership.

Chapter Summary and Lessons

ARM strove to bring the voice of the customer deeply inside the organisation in many ways. However, it would have been for nought if there was no motivation to listen and take note. The founding culture really helped here. Advanced RISC Machines had to engage with customers closely; else, it could have withered and died. It came down to personalities, too – people who demonstrated a customer and partner focus and led others to do the same.

When I first joined the engineering team in 1993, the person with the broadest influence was Tudor Brown, then Engineering Director. Tudor was passionate about the technology and ensuring the partners succeeded. John Biggs told me the story of Tudor receiving a message from Apple that they were having problems with their early system using ARM610 (Biggs, 2021). Tudor booked himself on a flight to California and reported to their reception the following day, US time. The Apple team were amazed and pleased that ARM's Engineering Director had flown immediately to work with them to investigate the problems. This behaviour rubbed off, and ARM built an

Engineering organisation that was very sensitive to partner issues, determined to ensure ARM's technology could be used successfully.

When an extra effort was required to get something delivered, or overseas travel was required, there was never a sense that a manager asked for this. We clearly understood that the partner's needs were pulling –hierarchical power was unnecessary. The partners provided the incentive and the motivation.

Being customer-focused will look different in different organisations with varying business models, but I believe some lessons from Arm are universally applicable:

1) **Sensitise the Organisation to Customers**. To be outwardly looking, the organisational purpose and goals should focus on its external impact – on people or an industry. The danger of only having financial goals is that they are inherently selfish and may lead to an inwardly looking outlook. Success should depend on close engagement with people and organisations outside the business.

2) **Look beyond immediate customers**. Who are your customers selling to? Engage with their requirements and understand how your product benefits them.

3) **Model the correct behaviour**. The leaders and colleagues in positions of influence must demonstrate customer focus and outwardly expect it from others. Walk the talk and show how actions back up the strategic plan.

4) **Distance to the customer**. Minimise the organisational distance and barriers between the people who have the

most impact on customer experience and the customer. What can be done to get the managers out of the way and connect development people directly?

5) **Many roads lead to Rome**. Create multiple mechanisms to understand the market and customer needs and directions. Ensure this information is piped directly inside the organisation.

6) **Operating structure**. Fan the flames of customer focus by building the operating structure to react and evolve to outside input. Day to day, week by week, how do people know what is needed by the customers and the business? And do they have the mechanisms to react and improve the products and services?

Five: Build a Delivery Machine

If the era of Robin Saxby as CEO was characterised by a start-up mentality, striving to establish ourselves in the market, how should we characterise Warren East's tenure?

Warren became CEO in October 2001 and retired from ARM in July 2013. In that time, the company's revenue grew from $213M to $1.118B; the number of employees from 772 to 2,833; and the number of ARM processors shipped by the partners from 420m to 10.4bn each year (ARM, Annual Report, 2001), (ARM, Annual Report, 2013). Warren's legacy as CEO was one of extraordinary growth, establishing ARM's processors in many new markets and broadening the product base to include Graphics processors and Physical IP. ARM established a reputation for the quality of its investor relations on the stock market and the ability to deliver strong financial results quarter after quarter.

ARM had some great opportunities in a time of industry growth and managed to scale – what's so special about that? I believe one answer is that ARM managed this while holding onto most of what made it successful in the first place. ARM maintained the right culture, stayed partner-focused and kept innovating, all while taking the difficult step of building an excellent delivery machine. ARM climbed higher and higher, but it wasn't easy and had many drivers. This chapter will explore some of the major factors that enabled this scaling without ARM losing its soul.

Building the operational excellence needed required separate but intertwined disciplines to be optimised. With the licensing business in full flight, ARM needed to be able to develop and deliver new products on an increasingly frequent heartbeat. The commercial organisation also needed to identify new opportunities and reel them in at an ever-increasing rate. A dedicated licensing function sits at the intersection of sales, legal, finance, and business divisions to ensure consistency, fairness, and delivered revenue. All these functions and systems had to be built and optimised to scale ARM's delivery machine. Let's focus on what I believe are four cornerstones of ARM's delivery machine:

Culture – Building a delivery focused organisation that took collective responsibility and was never satisfied.

Engineering Process – Building the engineering processes that provided reliable and high-quality product delivery.

Automation – Building methodologies that increasingly automated the creation, verification, and delivery of products; and automated the financial processes to support the business model.

Commercial Process – Building a commercial organisation and processes that took identified client opportunities and turned them into profitable signed contracts.

The payoff was huge – over the years, a relentless desire to do things better, to not accept the status quo, led to a culture of delivery – an execution machine that consistently delivered revenue and products for years on end, quarter after quarter.

The operating machine didn't come quickly. It all started from solid foundations and the belief that ARM could always do better, which drove us on and on.

1 – Culture

The 12 talented engineers from Acorn had a history of building highly optimised computer systems. Their work had been world-leading, with the Acorn Archimedes being the world's first RISC based computer for the home and educational markets when it launched in 1987 (Acorn RISCs it, 1987). And they had established some cultural habits, which were built upon and extended once in the new start-up environment.

Deliver for Apple or Die

Advanced RISC Machines' new microprocessor, the ARM610™, was commissioned for Apple's Newton MessagePad – and was the *raison d'être* for ARM's existence. It was to be challenging to complete the design in time with a still small team. By the middle of 1991, Lee Smith and Tudor Brown realised that at the current rate of progress, they were not going to meet the timescales demanded by Apple, and they were in danger of running out of money before it was complete (Howard, 2021). Not that the engineering teams had things easy as part of Acorn, but now they knew that the company would live or die by their personal efforts alone. They put in place a timesheet system to ensure everybody understood what needed to be completed every week if they were to succeed. The system kept everyone focused on the rate of progress and was the first of many small steps to create a delivery-focused engineering organisation. The ARM610 was first released for prototype manufacture in January 1992 and was ready for Apple to launch the production-ready Apple Newton MessagePad in August 1993. Their intervention had been decisive.

When I asked Lee Smith (Founder and Fellow of ARM) which cultural aspects most contributed to ARM's success, he told me of this time in the barn (Smith L. , 2022). He described the first two years as a difficult period where the "necessity to do what needed to be done... led to a strong culture of supporting one another". Lee said they didn't feel qualified to do what was needed and couldn't afford the people that were. Lee's summary was, "That was 'We, not I' years before we found that articulation."

With the FPA10 for Acorn taping out in 1992, too, and the financial lifeline of the GEC Plessey Semiconductor and Sharp Electronics licences by mid-1992, it was clear to the team that the extremely hard work and focus paid off. The organisation that I joined in 1993 had that hard-working mantra built-in.

Collective Responsibility

The early Acorn team had relied on what now seem like primitive tools to design and build the Acorn RISC Machine and its supporting chips. The opportunity for costly mistakes was high, and attention to detail was vital. One of the most enduring practices that the team created laid a foundation that continued beyond my leaving in 2018.

A logic designer, such as Tudor or Steve Furber, would write down their design requirements in a block specification, describing the purpose of a particular piece of functionality and the logical description. An Acorn VLSI engineer, like Jamie Urquhart or Dave Howard, would create the transistor level circuits and layouts to implement the block faithfully and within the constraints of speed, area, and power. Not an easy task. To improve the quality of the designs and to provide feedback, other engineers might be asked to review the paper block specs.

Harry Oldham, who had joined the VLSI team after the original ARM implementation, was (in)famous for his attention to detail and used a green pen to provide his written comments[26]. In this way, a designer would receive back several sheets of paper covered in green pen, asking difficult questions or pointing out mistakes and areas which couldn't be implemented efficiently. This process could be challenging but was highly effective. With honest and direct feedback, a designer was able to improve the design, the quality of the specifications and the chances of making errors in the final design much lower. It had the further benefit of spreading knowledge around the team so that they each became familiar with parts of the design outside their own area of expertise.

When ARM recruited a group of young graduates in 1994, I remember hearing the occasional "I've been green-penned" from those new to having their work reviewed by Harry. The reality behind the practice was two-fold: firstly, the designs were improved through challenge and questioning; secondly, less experienced engineers got the feedback they needed to learn and improve their craft. This method was total honesty and collective responsibility at work.

---

[26] According to Harry, Dave Howard had a red pen, Jamie Urquhart blue, and Jim Sutton a black one

Always Get Better

If you believe everything is fine, you aren't going to spend time looking for evidence to the contrary. You're probably not interested in spending time and energy improving your situation. However, if you think things are not acceptable, you're far more likely to look for ways to improve. ARM's foundation team and Robin came from organisations with uncertain futures – the people and technology may have been good, but the businesses had not thrived. They were determined to make ARM succeed yet knew they couldn't get everything right straight away – but they wanted to always get better.

Those who later joined ARM soon got a sense of the endeavour from their new colleagues. A desire to make this venture succeed, with a strong sense of not knowing everything we needed to know. John Biggs often spoke of us as "enthusiastic amateurs", which, for me, captured how things were: many things were done with as few resources as possible, just enough to make a great product. The team, of course, were highly professional with world-class skills. However, there were many things we didn't know – to coin the language of Donald Rumsfeld, there were many unknown unknowns.

ARM needed to build a powerful partnership of companies to ensure the ARM processor became an industry standard and produce extremely high-quality IP that partners could use worldwide. ARM made what was thought to be the right set of deliverables to support the IP, but feedback often told ARM that we hadn't done enough. For the first 10-15 years at ARM, I felt we were enthusiastic amateurs trying to do the right thing with inadequate knowledge. We were continuously self-critiquing with the desire to make things better. If we found something broken, great: let's fix it.

The culture of total honesty led inevitably to being our own worst critics. This sensitivity, combined with delivery to partners whose resources almost always were much more extensive than ours, led to a continuous need to improve. The timescales would always be challenging to achieve, the performance, power, and area targets would be just out of reach, and partners always hated bugs. ARM's technology has always been at the forefront of what is currently possible, and so our engineering activities would always need continuous honest appraisal and improvement. In my personal outlook, our work was "never good enough" – whereas some might prefer to say, "We can always do better."

"It's broken, let's fix it"

With many partners to service, the challenges multiplied, as each would give feedback on different elements of ARM's delivery. This was the candid feedback of partners in a challenging environment and always needed a competitive edge. ARM's role was to listen and understand the input and focus on the priority areas for improvement. When I asked Harry about ARM culture, he highlighted our willingness to listen to the partners (Oldham, 2022). He gave the example of ARM's macrocell layouts when TI told his team that they needed to shave 10% off the area of ARM7TDMI®[27]. At first, the VLSI

---

[27] TI were preparing for high volume manufacture of baseband chips for the mobile market. Every mm^2 of area cost them money

team at ARM couldn't see how this was possible, but after TI's insistence, the team were able to find new ways to layout the features and the targets were met.

ARM's performance was the result of collaboration internally and with the partnership. The environment helped create a healthy culture of "It's broken, let's fix it" – admittedly, this sat easier with the Cambridge culture than elsewhere.

No Blame Culture

If everyone's open and honest input has been taken into account, there will be a collective responsibility for the decisions taken, especially in a noisy and uncertain environment. If ARM were to succeed, it would have to be willing to fail; to try things, and learn lessons in a non-judgemental way. Even when struggling due to complexity or lack of knowledge, nobody called you an idiot. This mutual support for learning together on the spot allowed good ideas to emerge and flourish. That's not to say it was comfortable; I remember many occasions when my 'fantastic' idea or suggestion was shown to be less than fantastic. To maintain a totally honest culture takes resilience and an assumption of good intent. If people know each other very well and trust their intent, it's possible to listen and respect someone who criticises your proposals. If you're new to the company and someone senior tells you your idea is terrible for reasons a, b, and c, you will not necessarily enjoy the experience or thank them for it. It can be a demanding environment to get used to.

These cultural values were still firmly in place many years later. However, it took more and more effort to maintain. Newer employees, though, would see the good behaviour encouraged and the bad behaviour discouraged by colleagues. Fortunately, ARM had a lot of good role models.

In her book, *the fearless organization*, Amy C. Edmondson (Edmonson, 2019) promotes the creation of Psychological Safety to ensure workplaces can learn, innovate, and grow. In her view, "psychological safety is mission critical when knowledge is a crucial source of value". When you're in a situation where everyone's experience and knowledge are needed to help you navigate and succeed in an uncertain and complex environment, you had better ensure people feel safe to share information: the good, the bad, and the ugly.

At its best, I'm proud that ARM was using Psychological Safety years before most of us had even heard of the term.

2 – Engineering Processes

In June 1997, ARM had a "Stop the projects" day. The company had grown to a little under 200 people, and the business model was working. ARM had an increasing number of partners, a wide variety of products in development, and was also trying to win new customers by doing consultancy work. In Cambridge, ARM had long since outgrown the barn and moved back to the old Acorn site at Fulbourn Road. There was a steady increase in interest in ARM's products, and it already felt like a much bigger company than the one I joined.

Unfortunately, ARM had bitten off more than we could chew – it certainly wasn't through lack of hard work or talent. ARM was trying to do the right thing without all the knowledge or experience needed. The energy, commitment, and long hours were there, but we were trying to do too much without sufficient organisation. ARM needed a new way to manage its activities: which ones we prioritised and how we handled them. Above all else, ARM needed some project and portfolio management.

That day in June 1997, we weren't even sure what all the activities were or their status, so Simon Bates, the Engineering Manager, decided we would stop all the projects for a day to do a stocktake and some planning. We started to document what everything was, its status, and what was left to do – I believe it was a turning point for ARM. From that day onwards, the culture changed: we understood how important it was to manage the portfolio of projects more professionally and that we needed to grow and recruit dedicated Project Managers. ARM wanted to retain its enthusiasm but lose some of its amateurishness.

Project Lifecycle Management

Although there had always been some project management, it wasn't until Project Lifecycle Management (PLM) was formally introduced that ARM could effectively accelerate the development processes. The chip and IP development projects all tended to follow a similar waterfall flow, so a stage-gate approach was chosen with standardised names for the stages:

- Initial Investigation (II): The feasibility stage where there are many unknowns. The market requirements or technical research may still be in progress.

- Detailed Investigation (DI): The basic outline of the product is understood along with the target applications. This phase completes both the detailed specification and the detailed planning.

- Develop and Test (D&T): The design implementation is completed to the level of revision 0 – suitable for prototype silicon manufacture, but not necessarily the finished volume product.

- Trial: Additional testing by ARM and partners, leading to product revisions, if needed, and eventual project closure.

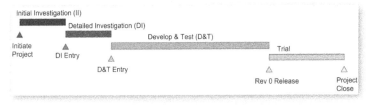

Waterfall Project Phases under ARM's PLM

With this standard naming for the project phases, ARM could communicate the status of project activities more reliably, both internally and externally. ARM's partners would gradually become familiar with this terminology, too, so we could align expectations of delivery. ARM could also now clarify the meaning of early releases of products to partners during D&T, with 'Development', Alpha and Beta releases, each with improved product characteristics – but importantly, not yet ready for manufacture.

These changes happened in the latter half of the 1990s, as the number of projects and products accelerated and allowed ARM to add further process improvements on top of PLM. Initially, we allowed project teams to choose for themselves whether to adopt this process. However, this *laissez-faire* approach changed as ARM took on more projects and staff. It was a difficult cultural challenge for an organisation used to more freedom to choose its processes.

Agile Thinking

The main drawback of Develop and Test (D&T) phase of PLM is that it is usually the longest part of an IP development project, yet has no intermediate milestones. This phase may last up to two years for an IP product development, and it is challenging to plan and make measurable progress with such a long phase. The tempting solution is to break down the implementation into a set of serial activities, each one completing before the next one starts. Estimate the length of each task, add them together and find out the expected length of the D&T phase. Job done.

Unfortunately, very few development types provide such clean handovers from one task to the next. As described in the Automation section of this chapter, in the second half of the 1990s, ARM was evolving to use a more modern set of tools and processes, which enabled a much higher productivity workflow. We took this opportunity to introduce a much more iterative approach to the developments.

Anyone involved with software development will be very familiar with 'Agile'. Software developers first published the Agile Manifesto in February 2001 (Manifesto, 2001). They aimed to break free from the constraints previously imposed on software projects by a 'waterfall' approach to development.

The 'Fasttrack' IP development methodology we were developing at the time was more akin to software development than the early ARM design methodologies. Although none of us had heard of the term 'Agile' in the context of engineering development, we understood we needed a much more iterative methodology. However, we needed this flow within the D&T phase of a 'waterfall' project, i.e., a hybrid approach.

John Biggs and I coined the term 'spiral design flow' to encapsulate our ideas. The approach taken was to break the D&T phase down into sub-phases, in each of which more of the required functionality was coded in a Hardware Description Language (HDL). At each sub-milestone, the HDL code (in whatever state of completion) was pushed through as much of the tools-based backend flow as possible.

So rather than wait until all the functionality was coded before trialling the first layout, we took early versions of the design, so-called Development Milestone versions, through the backend flow. The most significant sub-milestones were: Alpha, where the complete functionality had been coded, but verification was still very basic; and Beta, where the verification was essentially complete, but further 'soak' testing was required. Some projects had Development Milestones every two weeks, which pushed the current HDL code through the backend design flow. The team would then be able to measure progress against factors such as verification completeness, layout area, layout power consumption, processor performance, etc.

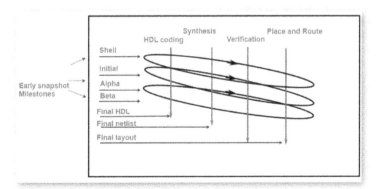

The Spiral Design Flow, Circa 1996

The spiral design flow was one of the significant process innovations in that period of ARM's evolution toward a reliable operating engine.

Framework

Anyone part of ARM Engineering from the late 1990s to as recently as 2016 would be familiar with the term 'Framework' – the implementation technology changed at least twice, but the concept remained in place. 'Framework' gave a single place for project process information to live, including stage-gate and release 'Assessments' completed by the Project Manager. A series of checklists (Assessments) were created for each stage-gate and release type to ensure the right level of due diligence. The Assessments would usually rely on a series of 'Review' checklists appropriate for the situation. A small team created the initial system in 1999, and it led to a steep improvement in the consistency of approach across the projects. The review questions would be updated based on experience to ensure future projects benefitted from previous learnings.

Framework was loved and loathed in equal measure for most of its existence. Some loved the 'all in one place' nature of the system, which allowed a new Project Manager to choose, for example, an "RTL design" template and then follow the assessments and reviews as they stepped through the project. Some loathed the fact that they had to answer multiple questions before anything could be released – why couldn't they just use their expert judgement to decide? Putting checklists in place does not allow people to turn off their brains but rather to nudge and spot areas they might have forgotten on each occasion. The comparable examples to use are those of a surgeon or airline pilot. Both are extremely experienced and skilled individuals, yet both use extensive checklists to ensure nothing is forgotten at crucial moments.

In my humble opinion, Framework was one of the most effective engineering processes we put in place to allow ARM to scale its operations across multiple projects and sites. The fact that it was largely accepted on rollout was a testament to the organisation's culture.

ISO9001

In 2001, ARM signed up to ISO9001 quality management to commit ARM to continuously improving its processes. A big part of ARM's system was based on the foundations of the PLM and Framework; however, we did not have precise descriptions of how the work needed to be carried out. Instead, we relied on employing technically competent people in the right roles and providing them with the training and mentoring needed for the work's highly dynamic and changing nature. When I was first introduced to ISO9001, I had assumed it would only work for manufacturing operations with repeatable activities. However, ARM demonstrated the benefit of using the process to continuously improve its systems, even when the underlying engineering processes and methodologies were changing almost constantly. ARM's implementation of IS9001 was one of its secrets of success. However, it would also be true to say it was viewed with deep suspicion by most engineers. Fortunately, the team responsible took great care to work with the project management community and not against it.

3 – Automation

Engineers founded ARM, and it has been a predominantly engineering-led organisation throughout its history. Engineers generally love automation; if there's an opportunity not to do a familiar task twice, they will jump on it. This mindset has many advantages, including reducing human error and the chance to move on to the next challenge. Add in the constant pressure to deliver a roadmap of new innovative products with limited growth in headcount, and it's clear that automation will always be a big part of ARM's journey.

Hard Macro Porting

In silicon IP terms, the early processors from ARM were all hard macros – they were delivered to partners as a black box with a known shape and size. ARM had already done the hard work of creating a fully working layout. All a partner needed to do was choose a position to place the block in their SoC and then connect power, inputs, and outputs. In the early 90s, this was a huge asset. One of the ARM IP selling points for the partner was receiving a known verified processor.

However, in that period, each semiconductor company had its own recipe for manufacturing silicon devices. Exact rules had to be followed for the transistor shapes and feature spacing. The differences between each partner's rules meant that ARM's hard macro needed to be modified for each partner and then verified to ensure it still functioned as intended.

As the number of partners grew and they migrated to new process rules, the range of process targets grew, too. Fortunately, the Acorn engineers had already built some flexibility into their designs, even though they worked with VLSI Technology alone. This flexibility was vindicated when, at one point, ES2 manufactured some chips for Acorn to help relieve some production problems VLSI Technology were having.

The challenge really took off with the success of ARM7TDMI in 1995, exposing ARM to an ever-increasing variety of process rules. If ARM were to scale the business, it would need to repeatedly port the design efficiently to multiple new partner processes. This period marked a frantic phase of effort to re-layout ARM7TDMI in an updated set of 'generic' rules and create a more automated set of methods to port, verify, and characterise the core on each process. If this all sounds painful, then you are right, it was. I'm not sure any company in history has ever had to port the same multi-thousand transistor design to so many different process technologies, from 1.2um down to less than 100nm. Eventually, the original ARM7TDMI design would be licensed to more than 200 partners and shipped in more than 10 billion silicon chips – it was worth the effort.

Fasttrack Design Flow and Texas Long Horns

One of the secrets of the original Acorn RISC Machine processor was the attention to detail of the low-level transistor implementation. This highly crafted implementation philosophy was the starting point for the team – a methodology that was part of their unique capability to produce a high-performance yet low-power microprocessor.

When it came to the control logic design for the CPU and the supporting chips, the methodology was biased towards higher productivity by using standard cell building blocks for the logic design. Nonetheless, using both phases of a clock and building some self-timed structures were some of the favoured techniques. At the time of the first SoC consultancy project ARM completed in-house, the ARM7500 for Acorn in 1993/4, the same methodologies were still being employed. Any difficulties the small project team of Graham Budd and I had could be overcome by talking to the original designers sitting a few desks away.

As ARM attempted to ramp up the number of SoC designs for the consulting efforts, we soon found it difficult to scale the specialist knowledge needed to use this essentially 'by-hand' methodology. The silicon manufacturing technology was marching forward, and the number of transistors that could be economically built into an SoC was rapidly increasing. The Electronic Design Automation (EDA) tools were advancing quickly, but they did so by simplifying some of the design rules. Many of the tricks used by ARM's engineers to reduce power and area were incompatible with these tools.

One of the last projects to use this highly optimised approach was building a very low power SoC for Psion, the ARM7100, in 1996. ARM chose to use an essentially new team based in Maidenhead for this consultancy – the challenges of the timescales, the requirements, and the design methodology nearly broke this highly motivated and skilled team. At one point, Tudor Brown slept on the floor overnight while helping the team with the design work. However, the result was a highly optimised low-power SoC, which enabled the Psion Series 5 product to operate off AA batteries for days and sleep for weeks on a penny-cell battery.

ARM needed partners to build the chips themselves to scale the business, and there was a deep sense of dissatisfaction with the design methodologies. From 1997 onwards, ARM embarked on a major activity to re-engineer many existing system components to be fully synthesisable and compatible with the latest automated EDA tools. ARM also upgraded the core interfacing standard (AMBA®) to be single edge and synchronous: Advanced High Performance Bus (AHB) was born. The new system IP components were branded Arm® PrimeCell™, and ARM also built the fully synthesisable ARM7-S™, ARM9E-S™ and ARM966E-S™ CPUs.

However, the industry was moving at different speeds, and some of ARM's partners, used to highly optimised designs, weren't convinced. ARM embarked on a piece of consultancy with Digital Semiconductor[28] in Texas. They expected ARM to deliver hand-crafted system design components to complement their StrongARM™ design for an SoC they were building (SA1100). ARM, however, was using many of the higher-productivity methodologies, in particular an automated way of distributing the internal timing signal (the clock). Digital had wanted to use full-custom 'Clock-o-matics'. At the final project review, Digital handed the ARM team a 6 feet wide set of Texas Long Horns, which they then had to get on the plane as hand luggage! Not something modern security rules would allow. In their view, ARM was a bunch of "cowboys" for cutting corners – in our view, it was the right way to go, and there was no turning back. An occasion when we listened to partner feedback but disagreed.

The 'Fasttrack' methodology enabled higher productivity consultancy with ARM's partners, and more of them were able to build ARM-based SoCs with only support services to help. ARM's IP quality had improved, partners were becoming much more familiar with SoC design, and we had enabled some

---

[28] Bought by Intel Corporation in 1998. Digital had developed a very high-performance ARM Instruction Set Compatible processor, called StrongARM

third-party design houses with ARM IP, too. Now the number of ARM-based SoC designs started to accelerate significantly. By the early 2000s, ARM effectively stopped doing SoC consulting, and most of the remaining consulting resources were redirected to IP product developments. ARM had successfully automated many of the design flow steps that previously were primarily completed by hand.

IP Delivery – 'Connect'

The complexity of IP delivery was an unexpected challenge of ARM's success: the number of partners rapidly increased to over 20 by early 1998. The number of unique IP products multiplied, and the number of individual parts for each product had exploded, too.

In 1995, when ARM delivered the ARM7TDMI product to TI for the first time, we had carefully put the design files on a computer server and given our contact at TI a password and instructions to download the files. The desire to keep the pace high was such that the TI engineer started the download on a Saturday morning from his office near Nice, France. Midway through, it all stopped, and I received a call from the engineer wondering what had happened. What had happened is that the power supply had cut at ARM's Cambridge office! The current approach had to change.

ARM needed to build a system that kept each product and all their parts available 24 hours a day, seven days a week, to partners worldwide. The system needed to support the ever-increasing number of products, parts, and partners, and it couldn't be subject to a single point of failure. A completely new system called 'Connect' emerged, which allowed ARM to automate the IP delivery process to the partners. As well as providing a 24/7 service, its most crucial role was to ensure that each partner could only access those products and parts that they had signed contracts for, along with providing an audit trail of the downloads. ARM repeatedly looked at commercial options to replace Connect in the subsequent years, but nothing came close to providing all the capabilities needed for many years. Connect allowed ARM to sign a contract a few minutes to midnight at the end of the quarter and give that partner access to the product nearly instantaneously. It really did "save the quarter" on some occasions.

The "revrec" Engine

The final automation element I will mention that played a significant role in enabling ARM's delivery operation is that of revenue recognition, or "revrec". The Generally Accepted Accounting Principles (GAAP) specify how revenue is recognised based on the contracts ARM has in play. As ARM grew, with multiple contracts with multiple partners covering dozens of products, the complexity of the task grew exponentially. Add in the challenge of products in development (allowing partial revenue recognition) and scenario planning of contracts under negotiation during a quarter, and it soon became nearly impossible to accurately judge the likely revenue for the quarter in advance.

Not surprisingly, there came a time when highly dedicated finance staff and brilliant spreadsheets would not give the information needed at speed. The 'Ascari' project was initiated to transfer the finance operations over to a suitable system, but most importantly, to allow the creation of a semi-automated "revrec" engine. The engine needs to consider the percentage completion and delivery status of IP product developments, the existing contracts, the expected contracts for the quarter and, of course, the latest GAAP rules. It was not enough to calculate after the end of the quarter. For ARM's delivery engine to function successfully, the team needed to know the likely revenue under different scenarios in near real-time. What would happen if ARM made the first beta-quality delivery of a new product? What if ARM put more engineering hours into completing more of product A versus B? What if ARM offered an incentive for a partner to sign a contract quickly? And so on.

The interaction of all these components demanded that ARM had automation in place and that large parts of the organisation were communicating exceptionally well as the quarter progressed. The sales, licensing, legal, and engineering teams all had to stay in sync to ensure ARM delivered the right contracts, products, and engineering effort every quarter.

4 – Commercial Process

In 2015, the full financial year before the SoftBank acquisition, ARM's revenue was $1,488.6, of which $587.9m was contributed from Technology licensing (ARM, Annual Report, 2015). That licensing revenue included some from the backlog[29] but a significant proportion from contracts signed that year. The commercial engine of the business could deliver over $100m of licensing revenue each quarter and also add to the future backlog.

The primary group leading the charge was, of course, the sales organisation, but they couldn't deliver contracts for

---

[29] Backlog represented previously signed contractual licence fees which could not be recognised in the quarter signed

signature without a commercially tuned legal department. Holding it all together and ensuring the business groups' goals were achieved was the licensing team. Although ARM partitioned the licensing team to align with the different business groups, they collaborated closely to ensure the proper value was assigned to all the IP and products in a contract. Their role was to represent the business groups' financial goals and help the legal team appropriately structure the terms for each type of product.

There would be tension in the system by its very nature, especially near the end of a quarter or financial year. A salesperson wanting to satisfy the partner and achieve their commission for the quarter. The legal team wanting to protect ARM's IP rights and against future risks. The licensing team wanting to preserve the value of the products and ensure each group meets its financial targets. As with so much about ARM's organisation, this engine resulted from years of optimisation and incredible collaboration across departments and geographies.

Business Review Meeting (BRM)

Bringing all this together each quarter was a monumentally challenging task that required calm but determined heads. The Chief Operating Officer led this meeting, most notably Graham Budd, from 2008 to near his retirement in 2021. The mechanism for coordinating the quarterly revenue challenge was the Business Review Meeting, the BRM, chaired by Graham.

This weekly event was the primary communication mechanism for the commercial organisation to understand the revenue goals, the current forecast revenue, the opportunities in play, and any blockers to progress. As you would imagine, the sophistication of the information available improved over the years but so did the scale of the challenge. One key role of the meeting was to ensure that each sales region was left in no doubt about their challenge for the quarter. Creating a sense of urgency but not fear was a delicate balance to strike. Looking at the charts at the beginning of each quarter would always be a sobering experience with a significant revenue gap. Still, gradually the gap would be filled as salespeople around the globe fought to turn opportunities into signed contracts and delivered products.

One of the challenging aspects of being a global operation was dealing with the cultural differences between the regions. In many ways, the British sat in the middle of the extremes. ARM's global sales lead in the early 2000s, Jerry Ardizzone, was from the US and joked about these cultural differences (and apologising for the stereotypes in advance, there is some truth in the following picture). On ARM's western edge were the very optimistic US team, who might be tempted to call a deal 'Green' when a contract hadn't even been drawn up; and on ARM's eastern edge were the very pessimistic Japanese team, who might call all their opportunities 'Red' until they had received a signed contract! So, unsurprisingly, a lot of levelling of inputs was needed to get an accurate view of the global commercial status.

The commercial operation at ARM was extremely professional and successful, and a testament to the culture at its best, working in deep collaboration with the rest of the organisation.

The Delivery Gene

In Chapter Three on Culture, I described how ARM's performance reviews included a rating of 50% for delivery and

50% for behaviour. It is important to highlight the 50% for delivery. ARM was an organisation with delivery to partners built into the DNA – it's what we did, and it's what we were each judged on at review time. There are many drivers of this that hopefully you can see described in this book. At his opening address to a Global Sales Conference, Warren East once said, "Things get done by doing." There's nothing hidden in this. It means what it says. ARM was an organisation where getting things done was expected and highly valued.

Chapter Summary and Lessons

From 2003 to 2015, Arm delivered increased dollar revenues every year (bar 2009)[30]: from \$229.3m to \$1,488.6m (ARM, Annual Report, 2003) (ARM, Annual Report, 2015). Profit before tax increased from £22m to £511.5m[31]. Licensing revenue grew from \$83.3m to \$587.9m, and Arm's north star metric of Arm-based chip shipments expanded from 782m to 15,000m units per year – nearly 28% compound average growth rate.

A company doesn't achieve those kinds of figures without doing many things well. The engineering development and IP delivery engines were executing on a scale we couldn't have imagined at the time of the IPO in 1998. The foundations Arm had laid with the right culture of continuous improvement, collaboration, and determination had successfully scaled the company. The strategy had been good, and industry trends were

---

[30] The year after the financial crash

[31] ARM often talked of revenue in dollars and profit in pounds, as it was dual-listed on NASDAQ and LSE until the Softbank acquisition

on Arm's side, but it was the ability to deliver and scale that enabled the excellent business outcomes.

What are the key lessons we can draw from this? It would be tempting to say "Culture, Culture, Culture", but with a bit more detail:

1) **Always Deliver (something)**. Arm felt there was no choice but to deliver something to customers and did whatever it took to do so. The teams rallied around to support each other to make this possible. It would always be possible to improve from there.

2) **Always get better**. The organisation grew a culture of dissatisfaction with the current status. We never felt our delivery processes or methodologies were good enough. There was a strong desire to continuously challenge and enhance the current working methods.

3) **Automation driven by the users**. Give the ownership and challenge to the business owners and operators closest to the challenges. They will often know which areas should be optimised and automated, and remain responsible for their continuous adaptation.

4) **Commercial Collaboration**. Arm's operations were global, and although each region and business group had a level of independence, this was held in check. The company's greater good was always to the fore, with a central organisation to ensure a 'good' deal in one location or group didn't undermine the collective whole.

Six: Admit When You're Wrong

When a strategy has served well, it's surprisingly difficult to let it go when things change. For an organisation to survive and thrive, it's vital to recognise when context changes, when the old tools and techniques are now, at best, a hindrance and, at worst, leading you to failure. We can all think of numerous examples of individuals or organisations where a failure to change has led to disaster. Kodak's failure to embrace digital cameras. Nokia's over-focus on the phone hardware instead of software. Or, more gruesomely, the cavalry charges at the beginning of the First World War. Why do people find it so difficult to change before it's too late? The new reality may challenge deeply held beliefs, or force writing off investments or, worst of all, pride to be swallowed by admitting the old way is no longer the best. It's tantamount to admitting you're wrong!

This chapter will explore three crucial moments in Arm's history where a change of direction was needed, but internal and external voices resisted. The status quo in each case had powerful logic, so I'll explore the cultural and organisational elements that created the environment for taking the right course eventually. Acknowledging the teaser of the chapter title, this is less about people being wrong and more about recognising when the context has changed and being able to change direction before it's too late.

Customer-focused organisations position themselves to sense the messages of the market. However, organisations also need to have a culture of listening, debating, and action to benefit fully. I believe Arm performed very well on the first metric, and events show it did a good job on the latter, too. As the examples of this chapter show, even when the forces of resistance or reluctance were high, time and time again, Arm managed to shift perspective and action an updated strategy. Arm has been especially good at admitting when things need to change – at "waking up and smelling the coffee". The roots of this were probably born in the "brutal honesty" mantra of the founding team (Saxby, 2021).

"Brutal" Honesty

Without brutal honesty, your organisation won't understand the harsh reality.

When Stalin's Soviet Union was at its darkest hour with Hitler's forces bearing down on Moscow, he turned to General Alexei Antonov, his trusted Chief-of-Operations. At the daily briefings, the latter would always tell Stalin precisely the situation on the ground: the good, the bad, and the ugly (Overy, 1995). There was no attempt to give Stalin only the good news – it was critical that the bad news was also heard and understood. Even the despot Stalin realised that in the most dangerous of situations, you have to know the harsh reality of the situation to plan your way out successfully. This was only possible due to the brutal honesty of Alexei Antonov.

When Robin joined the team from Acorn in 1990, they knew they had a big challenge in front of them. The team realised that if they were to work together effectively in this new and emerging environment, they would need to be as honest and open as possible. Something that Jamie Urquhart called "total honesty". By being totally honest with each other, they would be able to understand each other's concerns and address them quickly. No one person had all the answers; they needed to pool their knowledge and ideas to determine the best way forward. The ex-Acorn team knew each other very well and also accepted Robin into that team. They trusted the good intent of the others even when they disagreed, and they had a view that everyone's input was equally welcomed – there was no unnecessary sense of hierarchy.

With a flat hierarchy and total honesty, the foundations were laid to enable ARM to deal with the challenges ahead, even when the facts attacked firmly held beliefs. The "brutal" bit of "brutal honesty" had to be gradually toned down with time and additional people to become more emotionally aware. However, most of the essential elements of the culture were retained. The object of debates and discussions was the issue itself. I cannot remember a time when an individual was attacked for expressing an opinion or view. Openness and challenge were the norm, as distinctly uncomfortable as they can be. We debated, we disagreed, we understood other perspectives and then agreed on a way forward. A better way ahead was almost always uncovered through the complete honesty of the approach.

Along the way, some significant turning points marked ARM's journey to billions of CPUs. If ARM hadn't managed to challenge the incumbent wisdom of the day and face up to reality, the story might well have been very different. The first example is the most well-known among the ARM community, that of the Thumb®-based processor, ARM7TDMI®. As the story illustrates, it was not as straightforward as it seems in retrospect. Adding a new capability to an already highly competent product opened a raft of new applications and won some key design wins. The design win at Nokia Mobile Phones was the seed that enabled ARM to establish a market-leading position with over 95% of the world's phones in 2021 using one or more ARM-based processors. The Thumb innovation happened only by allowing the feedback of customers to overturn the wisdom of the day. Ironically, by cracking open access to this deeply embedded application, the mobile phone market led, step by step, to ARM's processors eventually taking on the high-performance processors needed for smartphones, then tablets, then laptops, and eventually to servers and even supercomputers. An unexpected way to the top.

The second example was a significant change in design methodology for the CPUs: exclusively using synthesis tools to generate the gate level implementation from a high-level description. The first ARM-based CPUs were built with handcrafted circuits for the most critical logic to achieve the desired performance, area, and power consumption. By 1997, most SoC logic was being built with synthesis for productivity, but surely this didn't make sense for the highly optimised CPU core itself?

The final example highlighted here is the microcontroller market and the Cortex®-M series of CPUs. In this case, the established wisdom to be overturned was the success of the ARM7TDMI CPU itself – a challenge of ARM's own making. Why build a CPU without backwards compatibility when this had served ARM so well to date?

The Story of Thumb

'Thumb' is the name of the project and instruction set extension to the ARM7™ CPU, which ARM initiated in 1994. It was a revolutionary step that transformed the company's prospects by opening a new realm of embedded opportunities. The innovation famously enabled the ARM7TDMI CPU to win sockets at Nokia Mobile Phones for their new GSM phones and, perhaps less well known, at Nintendo for their Gameboy Advance™. Before deciding to go ahead with this extension, the ARM7 struggled to shine in applications with limited memory and deeply embedded systems. Yet there was some resistance to change. The processor seemed ideal for many applications where high-performance with low power was vital. ARM's limited resources had been expended building the ARM7DMI™[32], which was only just being marketed, so why did anything need to change now?

This is the story of an outsider who dared to challenge the current orthodoxy. Crucially, after nearly losing those two key design wins, ARM finally listened and acted.

Robin's impact as an outsider to the ex-Acorn team was commercial and inspirational. The next outsider to significantly impact Advanced RISC Machines in those early days was a Computer Science Master's graduate from Canterbury University, New Zealand. His impact was to be deeply technical. Dave Jaggar had recently completed his Master's thesis: "A Performance Study of the Acorn RISC Machine". He emailed it, along with his CV (Resumé), to Advanced RISC Machines in February 1991 (Jaggar, 2021). In a story of the one that nearly got away, he heard nothing for three months, then tried again, along with an email to MIPS Inc, too. Fortunately, the next day he got a response from Lee Smith, the Software Manager,

---

[32] An ARM7 with Debug, fast Multiplier and 'ICEbreaker' logic

replying that they were indeed looking for a software engineer. After a late-night telephone call, ARM offered Dave a job, and he arrived in Cambridge, UK, in June 1991.

He was welcomed with open arms into the ARM family, with Mike Muller giving him an immediate place to stay in his own house. Soon after, Dave found a place to stay, and Robin rented a room from Dave for his visits to Cambridge during the week. The two Cambridge outsiders found themselves together: one the CEO; the other a newly arrived graduate engineer. They had a lot in common, including sharing the same birthday, albeit 20 years apart. Most importantly, they got along; neither is quiet nor retiring – they spoke their minds. As Robin told me, they were able to short circuit many things from the top to the bottom of the organisation. Dave's view was that Robin had the vision of what needed doing (global RISC standard) and then got out of his way (Jaggar, 2021).

After some time building an Instruction Set Simulator for the development tools and software for the development boards, Dave found himself to be the only person in the company who had a good knowledge of the inner workings of the ARM core – Sophie Wilson and Steve Furber[33] having not joined ARM. With most of the resources dedicated to Apple or Acorn projects and software tools, Dave was now ARM's de facto core architect one year after graduating.

Dave's Master's thesis had given him a software designer's view of the ARM processor, and now he had the hardware view, too. He specified some debug and multiplier extensions to the

---

[33] Sophie and Steve were the original architects of the ARM processor in Acorn Computers

ARM6™ processor, leading to the ARM7DMI processor. The latest licensee (TI) wanted to use this core in embedded applications alongside their proprietary technology. Except that Dave heard the same message on almost every customer visit. For deeply embedded applications, the ARM core's performance was excellent, the power consumption fantastic, and the die size was perfect, but…

Designed on a small budget, the original ARM processor would never compete on absolute performance with the high-end cores from Intel, Motorola, Digital, and others. In the mission to become the global RISC standard, the choice to focus on the embedded market rather than computing was the right one. However, was this 6502-inspired processor fit for purpose?

Dave Flynn had joined Dave Jaggar in the technical marketing team and explained that during his time in Active Book Company (Flynn, 2021), they had found the ARM processor code used a lot of memory compared to most CISC processors. Dave Flynn had done some software experiments to compress the ARM instructions, thus saving costly memory chips. Although the ARM core was one of the most code-efficient 32-bit RISC processors available, the code size seemed large compared to 8-bit or 16-bit instruction processors.

Furthermore, the ARM CPU relied on a 32-bit wide memory delivering instructions every cycle to achieve its performance. The RISC mantra aimed to keep the core simple and the performance high but relied on fast memory. The ARM team discovered from prospective customers that deeply embedded applications often had much smaller memory systems to keep cost and area under control. Fetching 32-bit instructions and data from 16-bit or even 8-bit wide memory slowed the processor to a crawl. Dave Jaggar was, at this point, visiting a lot of customers and porting their code to the ARM processor for benchmarking and seeing a regular pattern. In Dave's words, the "RISC is simpler" story fell apart when they tried to build a memory system. It seemed that the RISC-based ARM CPU wasn't so suited to embedded applications after all. Dave was, in effect, calling into question the strategy of pushing their 32-bit RISC-inspired processor into these applications. However, this isn't a message the business would have been keen to hear, having invested their limited resources in the ARM7DMI for embedded applications.

Nintendo and Nokia Tip the Scales

Dave Jaggar explained that he was working in an environment where they were all trying to make their current solution work. ARM needed new design wins and licence deals, and delaying them to the 'next' design would just slow time to revenue. The apparent loss of two major opportunities tipped the scales in favour of change.

TI was hunting for a design-win with the ARM processor. They had pitched it to Nokia as a baseband controller, alongside their DSP technology for Nokia's next-generation GSM mobile phone. This design win would be a massive volume opportunity for TI's DSP and the ARM processor. However, the feedback from Nokia was that the code density wasn't good. Dave believes there was a bit of disbelief by some of the ARM team.

Soon after, on 14th January 1994, Dave found himself in Japan for a meeting with Nintendo. ARM's early licensee Sharp took Robin, Mike, and Dave to meet their significant customer. It was a big deal to be meeting such a large OEM with the licensee. Sharp supplied chips with an 8-bit processor for the highly successful Nintendo Gameboy™, and they wanted to be the supplier for the successor, the Gameboy Advance™. It was crucial for Sharp, so they wanted to take ARM's CEO with them. Nintendo wanted 32-bit performance, but the code size of the ARM core would kill their margins as the games were sold as cartridges containing memory chips. Here was the code density challenge spelt out in front of the ARM team. The current 32-bit ARM processor just wasn't good enough in this embedded application.

That weekend, the ARM team had planned to go skiing together, and as they sat on the Shinkansen from the Nintendo visit towards Matsumoto, Dave sketched out a possible solution for Robin and Mike. With the recent news from Nokia and now Nintendo ringing in their ears, they understood something had to change. Dave had wondered what would happen if you recoded some instructions into 16-bit space only using the most frequently used instructions. As each instruction was half the size, not only might the code density be much improved, but the performance from restricted memory systems should be higher too. Then, emboldened by the conversation and still on the same train, he hacked a version of the ARM tools to test the theory with some example programs. Result: the code size might be ~35% smaller and run significantly faster from 16-bit memory. His lightbulb moment was to propose that the 16-bit instruction set was an addition rather than a replacement. They could take the ARM7DMI and keep backwards compatibility with 32-bit ARM instructions for when performance was essential and wide memory was available (e.g., on-chip). And use the 16-bit instructions for narrow memory and where code density was paramount. With tongue firmly in his cheek, Dave suggested Thumb as the codename for the reduced footprint instruction set: "It's the useful wee bit on the end of your arm."

The initial analysis stood up to finer inspection back in the office. With permission given to discuss the idea further, Thumb was disclosed to TI and selected potential customers. Acorn, however, was not keen. Robin explained that at the ARM Holdings board meeting, Apple gave the deciding vote to allow ARM to proceed despite Acorn's resistance. Acorn feared the loss of code compatibility for their products, among other concerns. The mindset that had helped create the Acorn RISC Machine in the first place (with the clear computer system advantages that their simple but powerful core provided) had been holding ARM back.

The radical change had needed the powerful motivation to find new business, hearing multiple outside voices questioning the current solution and someone not held back by the past.

Dave pushed forward, seeking feedback from customers and partners. Just three weeks after the fateful train journey from Nintendo, on 8th February 1994, he visited Nokia in Oulu, Finland. What he and Pete Magowan, the European Sales lead, initially heard was not good. Nokia had already dismissed the ARM-based option, as initial benchmarking showed it running more than 50% slower than their existing solution running from 8-bit memory. Additionally, the code size was too big. They had shortlisted three processors for further evaluation, and ARM7DMI was not on the list.

Here, perhaps, was the most significant diving catch in ARM's history. They told Nokia about their ideas for the new 16-bit instruction set and promised to get Nokia some data by mid-March on "what it would do for their code density" to keep the ARM processor on the table (Jaggar, 2021). When Nokia found out more, according to Dave, they more or less said, "If you can deliver to our timescales, then you've got the business." They clearly believed that the 32-bit performance RISC processor, with 16-bit code density, joined with the TI DSP, would give them a lead on Motorola and Ericsson, their arch-rivals in the growing mobile phone market.

"If you can deliver to our timescales, then you've got the business"

Although it was perhaps the opportunity to win the Nintendo business that persuaded the ARM holdings board to support the Thumb programme, the Nokia design-win drove the timescales. ARM now had to move very fast to implement Thumb in the ARM7.

The ARM7TDMI was born

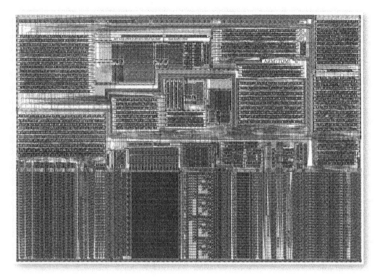

1995 ARM7TDMI

The plan was to minimise the risks by touching as little of the existing ARM7DMI design as possible. The strategy paid off: our relatively small team, led by Simon Segars (later CEO), was able to tape out and demonstrate a working ARM7TDMI test chip in late 1994. The new Thumb extensions worked the first time, building confidence with TI and, crucially, Nokia. TI designed the core into a chip called MAD (Microprocessor and DSP), which became the central controller of Nokia's early GSM phones, the first of which was the famous Nokia 8110 banana phone used by Keanu Reeves to save the world in *The Matrix*.

Synthesisable Processors

For full disclosure, in the example of the 'Tiger' development described in this section, I was part of the leadership team that approved the development decisions. So, I was part of the 'problem' and part of the solution. The capability of the synthesis tools improved much faster than many inside the group realised at the time. In the end, the semiconductor and ecosystem partners pulled ARM to the final position – ARM sensed the mood music had changed and responded.

The Acorn RISC Machine had a lot of highly optimised, handcrafted circuitry to ensure the implementation was as low power as possible. The handcrafted[34] logic in processor designs was usually focused on the highly repetitive and timing-critical parts of the design: the arithmetic and logic unit (ALU)[35] and the registers[36]. These elements are called the 'datapath' of a processor. The CPU also contains a lot of general control logic implemented using standard logic gates for implementation efficiency. Acorn had also used a home-grown tool to generate certain logic blocks more efficiently – PLA decoders. This mixed semi-custom and full-custom design methodology was used in all the subsequent CPU core designs up to ARM7TDMI and the cached cores built with it, ARM720T™ and ARM740T™.

With the improvements in the EDA tools for logic synthesis during the 1990s, the initial ARM8™, ARM9™ and ARM10™ CPU developments used a Hardware Description Language to

---

[34] full-custom as it's known
[35] the ALU is where computation happens
[36] the local values used by the ALU

design and simulate the design. Then the control logic was synthesised to gates, whereas the datapath was still built using the full-custom approaches. The high-performance processor design community strongly believed that a processor datapath needed to be handcrafted to achieve the necessary performance, power, and area (PPA) characteristics. And many of ARM's processor designers felt the same way.

In 1997, the success of ARM7TDMI attracted many new licensees, including potential ones who wanted a synthesisable version to use in their fully synthesised ASIC design methodologies. A fully synthesisable version would simplify many elements of the overall SoC development, even though it might result in inferior PPA for the CPU itself. Simon Watt and Dave Flynn started the synthesisable ARM7 project in collaboration with Synopsys, and in 1998, the ARM7TDMI-S™ was ready for its first licensee, National Semiconductor.

Dave explained (Flynn, 2021) that, by 1997, many inside ARM considered the ARM7 to be an inferior processor, so a synthesisable version was acceptable because it was older and relatively small. The ARM9TDMI™ core was nearing completion, and some suggested that a fully synthesisable version of this be produced next. There was resistance from those who felt strongly that the PPA would be compromised too much. However, Dave was meeting increasing numbers of partners who thought that the improvements in productivity and flexibility of a fully synthesisable core far outweighed the perceived downsides. A combination of partner pull and internal push enabled the go-ahead of the synthesisable ARM9. The internal push was also the opportunity to add additional instructions, the 'E' DSP extensions, into a synthesisable core development. This feature may have cost too much to put into the full-custom ARM9 core. Two parallel ARM9 developments then occurred: ARM920T™ using the ARM9TDMI core in 2000; ARM9E-S™ and ARM966E-S™ in 1999, ARM946E-S™ in 2000 and ARM926EJ-S™ in 2001. These were early skirmishes in a 'battle' fought for a few more years.

The ARM10 development underway in the Austin, Texas, office saw a similar tug-of-war. The ARM1020E™ with full-custom datapath was completed in 2001, but by popular demand was followed up with the synthesisable ARM1026EJ-S™ in 2002. With increasing acceptance, many CPU micro-architects in ARM could see the massive productivity improvements, and the relative ease of adding new core features, such as Arm® Jazelle®, meant that fully synthesisable cores were the way forward. The ARM11™ cores delivered from 2002 onwards were purely synthesisable from the start.

One final roll of the dice was left. The 'Tiger' development, started in 2002 in Austin, needed to provide a significant step-up in performance relative to ARM11. The 'Tiger' core would have a 13-stage pipeline with dual-issue instruction execution and all the latest architectural features, including Arm® Neon™ for even better data processing capability. In short, it was to be the biggest and most powerful CPU ARM had designed to date. The CPU micro-architects were determined that it had to be built with full-custom datapaths. And most of the potential licensees agreed. It had to be competitive with Intel's XScale™ range, so they pushed for this methodology, too. However, the development cost might have made ARM's licensing model unviable, with royalties too distant to be meaningful in the business plan.

The compromise was the 'Charles de Gaulle' strategy, proposed by Simon Segars, named after the architecture of that airport in Paris: a central hub with several terminals off to the sides. ARM would focus on the processor functionality and its own high-performance implementation, allowing the lead partners to develop their own optimised datapaths to the template delivered by ARM. In short, this was not a fully synthesisable development, but the high-level model was written in a way that almost allowed it.

The Cortex-A8™, as Tiger was named, was delivered in 2005 and was a success. However, the licensees' implementation investment was high, and pull arrived from new potential licensees and the EDA vendors to produce a fully synthesisable version. Again, ARM collaborated with the EDA vendors, who helped us ensure the design was fully compatible with their tools. The fully synthesisable Cortex-A8 was created. No, it didn't have quite the same performance, power, or area characteristics of a full-custom implementation. Still, when a new, better silicon process was used, the differences didn't appear to warrant the additional effort.

Finally, the tide had entirely gone out on full-custom cores by ARM; from then on, all ARM CPU cores were fully synthesisable from the start.

Synthesisable CPUs Postscript

As ARM transitioned to delivering the CPU IP as synthesisable products, it became clear that many silicon partners still did not have the resources or experience to deal with this new type of product. They wanted the flexibility to use different configurations[37] and different manufacturing processes but

---

[37] For example, different memory/cache sizes, or with Floating point accelerator

lacked the skills to create high-performance and low-power implementations for themselves. ARM provided an implementation (hardening) consultancy service to those partners for this transitional period, helping them get the best possible solutions for their SoC designs. However, this wasn't a scalable situation, so we encouraged an ecosystem of third-party implementation consultancies and collaborated with the EDA vendors to create reference methodologies to help the silicon partners without ARM's direct involvement.

Microcontrollers

A microcontroller (MCU) is a small computer on a chip with built-in memory and input/output peripherals. They are designed to be very low cost, as versatile as possible, and sell into thousands of different applications: from washing machines to electric window motors in cars.

In 2002, the year before ARM decided to focus on the microcontroller market, about 70% of the total processor sales by volume were for 4- and 8-bit processors (Turley, 2002). These low-performance processors were used in enormous volumes because they are very low cost and simple to use and program. If an ARM processor were to significantly impact this market, it would need compelling benefits to justify any additional silicon costs.

The Thumb innovation had enabled ARM processors to become viable solutions in deeply embedded markets where 32-bit performance was required but needed low-cost memory systems. The ARM7TDMI was already extremely popular, with hundreds of design wins. It provided upward compatibility for software, both operating system and user code, to the other more powerful ARM processors of that era: the ARM9, 10, and 11 processors.

In 2003, ARM fully committed to a strategy to increase its partners' share of the 16- and 32-bit microcontroller markets. Some ARM partners had already released microcontroller products based on ARM7TDMI. Though, these chips were priced in the $5+ bracket rather than $1 or below where the volumes lay. Could a 32-bit processor really ever be viable in sub-$1 chips?

The success of the ARM7TDMI in winning low-end embedded applications almost certainly blinded ARM to what was needed further down the complexity curve. Significant change would require overcoming internal resistance to not using ARM7TDMI.

Paul Kimelman had joined in 1997 after ARM purchased his small debug tools company and was a fierce proponent of the microcontroller market. Paul told me (Kimelman, 2021) how he had approached Tudor Brown with his ideas for an ARM processor targeting this market. Tudor encouraged him to work with the marketing team and partners using ARM7TDMI. In Paul's view, the partners were excited by his ideas, but some in Cambridge were less keen on the radical changes being proposed – it would break strict code compatibility with ARM7TDMI. This idea seemed a step too far. The success of ARM7TDMI led to a proposal for a much lighter touch change. This decision seems an entirely rational response given the success of that product to date. At the 2003 ARM Partners' Meeting, the modified ARM7 product was presented to partners to get their feedback. Unfortunately, the partners largely rejected this proposal for not helping to drive down the simplicity and silicon cost sufficiently to enable truly low-cost MCUs to be built.

In classic "if you don't believe me…" style, Paul and his colleague in the US office built their more radical ideas into a simple prototype system to demonstrate what would be possible. Once the not-so-secret skunkworks was discovered, he was encouraged to write up a set of slides with "deep details" for the ARM Architecture Group (AAG) to review. The AAG couldn't find anything radically wrong with the proposals, so the Sandcat project to build the new CPU was initiated after further evaluation and refinement. The time was right for a refresh of ARM's processor branding, too, and Sandcat became the Cortex-M3™ processor, launched in 2004 – part of the broader Arm® Cortex® processor brand and shipped in over 25bn chips to date.

The specification for this product marked a departure from operating system compatibility with ARM7TDMI. It also contained numerous other changes to directly target efficient operation in deeply embedded microcontroller markets. As well as significantly simplifying programming, the design would allow extremely low pin count MCU devices. This approach was exactly the right thing for the microcontroller market. Still, ARM had to swallow hard to move away from the mindset that the ARM7TDMI was the product suitable for the lowest cost markets and that strict operating system compatibility was needed.

As of mid-2022, there are 11 products in the Cortex-M range of processors, described by Arm as "Low-power processors for microcontrollers and constrained, energy-efficient applications" (Cortex-M, 2022). Building on the success of ARM7TDMI, the Cortex-M CPUs are Arm's most licensed cores and have been built into thousands of chip designs, shipping more than 13 billion units in 2020 alone. Every major MCU vendor globally has at least one range of Cortex-M based products, and low-cost development boards are standard teaching tools for hundreds of university courses. The Cortex-M processors indeed are the de-facto standard for 32-bit microcontrollers.

Chapter Summary and Lessons

Other examples could have been described where, in each case, internal inertia and "what's worked well until now" had to be fought and overcome. Sometimes the inertia was overcome by the injection of outside people, and sometimes by market pressure and fear of failure. The critical point is that Arm did listen and did respond. The ARM7TDMI, and later the Cortex-M3 developments, were both game-changing for the markets they were targeting – both leading to significant uptake of the products and an opening up of opportunity. Fully synthesisable processors offer such significant productivity and flexibility benefits that today, nobody could imagine delivering Arm's processor or system IP any other way. All advancements faced internal resistance initially, but Arm's customer focus, its culture of open and honest debate, and an urge to succeed led to the necessary change of direction. Arm "woke up and smelt the coffee".

The key lessons for organisations:

1) **Gather the feedback**. Organisations need feedback from customers and the market – open the channels of information flow. Test your ideas with the market, listen

to and challenge the input to understand it fully. Ensure people with deep understanding hear the feedback and are motivated to respond.

2) **Amplify the messages**. Even when customers or the market are giving clear signals, sometimes it's possible to discount them if the messages don't fit the organisation's narrative. In Arm, it sometimes needed dissenting voices who could 'see' things differently and had the skills to persuade their colleagues. These voices need cultivating and amplifying.

3) **Don't shoot the messenger**. Organisations need to be as objective as possible. Unadulterated facts are necessary if an effective debate is to happen. The chances of success are higher when you really understand the situation and what's needed. Arm's foundational culture of total honesty helped immensely.

4) **Hold your pride lightly**. Once you understand what needs to change, it is time to let go of pride in the current approach. It used to work, but time has moved on. The King is dead. Long live the King.

5) **Move fast**. Once the new way forward is clear, run with it, engage with customers to create pull, and drive it towards success. Demand a pace that gives little time for doubts to linger.

Seven: Create an Ecosystem of Shared Success

"It is not from the benevolence of the butcher, the brewer, or the baker, that we expect our dinner, but from their regard to their own interest," wrote Adam Smith in his famous book *The Wealth of Nations* (Smith, 1776). Much has been extrapolated from Smith's book, but it's important to acknowledge that he was writing towards the end of the 18th century. A time when most business enterprises were small, family-owned, and operating very locally. The pursuit of self-interest by the butcher or the baker did indeed put food on the table for the local society. Fast forward over 200 years to the era of large global corporations, it's arguable whether that same self-interest will always have a positive impact. More care and intent are needed to ensure that what's good for the shareholders is also good for the employees, customers, the environment, and society.

Of course, Advanced RISC Machines had self-interest at the heart of their goals and strategy. However, the original business model and plan were structured towards a mutual interest in success with partners. The team knew that with few resources, the only way to create sufficient revenue to fund future developments was to enable other, often much larger, companies to make even more revenue based on ARM's technology. The licensing and royalty model enables access to complex and valuable IP for a fraction of the up-front development costs, and royalty is only paid when chips are sold.

To say ARM's self-interest is good for society is a bit of a stretch, but is ARM's self-interest good for the industry? Quite probably. Such is the nature of processor IP that creating an ecosystem that supports a microprocessor reduces risks and costs for the industry. More than that – a thriving processor ecosystem will also enable significant opportunities for the partnership. Such an ecosystem allows SoCs to be made for applications that would not have been previously economically viable or even possible. Applications such as the smartphone in your pocket, your automated central heating system, or the Smart TV in your lounge.

ARM's goal to be a global RISC standard would only succeed if an ecosystem of partners were created that could work for the good of the OEMs and end-users. This ecosystem of partners for a CPU will include compatible system IP, software development tools, hardware emulation systems, ported operating systems and optimised software libraries. There are far too many complex elements required to create an end-product for ARM to try to do it all. ARM's early partnership focus was on the semiconductor manufacturers but widened from there. In some cases, the time from development to significant revenue was multiple years, and ARM needed to take a long-term approach to relationships.

ARM's approach to building the ecosystem of partners was based on mutual respect and long-term shared success. We wanted to acknowledge each other's contributions and collaborate to solve the complex challenges ahead. The reason may have been self-interest, but the method was to seek opportunities for shared success.

Semiconductor partners

When Advanced RISC Machines talked about "the partnership", it was heavily focused on the semiconductor partners, the companies that paid ARM licence fees and royalties. In March 1998, the picture of the partnership on the ARM website looked like this:

Advanced RISC Machines' Partnership, March 1998

To be the global RISC standard, it was essential to have partners from all the major semiconductor regions who represented as many different markets as possible. ARM's goal was for partners to complement one another: supplying their special sauce to the markets. This situation would be good for their revenue and ours, too.

Part of the unwritten contract with our semiconductor partners was that ARM would treat them fairly. As Tudor used to say, if asked who ARM's favourite partners were, "It's a bit like asking which is your favourite child." The correct answer is that ARM didn't pick winners among the partners. However, they often had different competencies and capabilities.

When ARM became a leader in markets like mobile phones, we were sometimes asked: "Why don't you charge more for royalties?" The answer is balance and fairness – it wouldn't make for a good long-term partnership. There must be a balance of return for the companies involved and fairness in the risk and reward. ARM needs to pay for the ever-increasing complexity of IP development and provide investors with a return. Those costs can occur years in advance of the possible returns. For example, the Armv8 64-bit architecture development started actively in 2006, was announced in 2011, and the first chip shipments started in 2013. ARM's partners also need to be able to sell chips profitably into the market – they need to balance their development and manufacturing costs. If the royalty is too high, ARM-based chips will price themselves out of the market. And there will always be alternatives, either in-house proprietary or competitive IP vendors.

The result of this balance and fairness is that royalties work out at "a few cents" on average across all the applications, including the highest volume, lowest cost microcontrollers. Partners need to sell a lot of chips for ARM to receive significant revenue. Not just tens of thousands, but millions. A few million multiplied by "a few cents" starts to add up; a billion spread across multiple partners multiplied by "a few cents" is meaningful.

The promise of significant royalty revenue was a distant dream in the first few years of the company's existence. ARM would have to survive on licensing, tools, services fees, and some research grant funding. To scale, the company needed multiple partners to get into volume production. In 2004, the number of ARM-based CPU chips sold exceeded one billion for the first time; it was the first year that royalty revenue reached parity with licensing revenue – the 14th full year of operation after foundation. Royalties are a long game – and were far from assured in the early to mid-90s.

ARM spent a lot of time with semiconductor companies, presenting roadmaps, understanding their needs, and promoting ARM's products. As with any meaningful relationship, building the necessary openness and trust can take time. However, this was the default position that ARM took with partners. ARM wanted a long-term relationship based on mutual understanding and trust to ensure shared success.

"Part of the unwritten contract with Arm's semiconductor partners is that that we will treat them fairly"

OEMs[38]

In the simpler times of 1990, OEMs bought silicon devices from semiconductor vendors. They were ARM's partners' customers. When Apple invested in Advanced RISC Machines, they did so to ensure the technology could be integrated into SoCs, which they bought from the semiconductor manufacturers. The growth of the Foundry silicon manufacturers has since blurred the lines, but to understand Arm's approach to the ecosystem, let's use the term OEM to mean the end purchasers of silicon chips who built them into their products.

OEMs in many markets are very powerful. They bear the cost of marketing to consumers and understanding their needs. They, therefore, tend to exert power in their purchasing of components and technologies for their products. Arm's semiconductor partners most often sell to the OEMs, and winning a contract with a particular OEM can be make or break for one of their business groups.

What was the best strategy for Arm to employ in this scenario?

For much of Arm's existence, the OEMs might buy some software development tools directly from Arm, although not semiconductor IP. They relied on the semiconductor vendors to offer them silicon that could provide the functionality they needed to give them a competitive advantage in the marketplace. When Nokia Mobile talked to Texas Instruments

---

[38] Original Equipment Manufacturers, e.g. Apple or BMW or Samsung

about supplying a chip for their new generation digital cellular phones, they wanted something that would give them an edge. A 32-bit processor would provide a better-quality mobile experience for users through improved performance versus the 8-bit and 16-bit processors they had used to date.

We believed that by using a standard processor, like Arm's, an OEM would be able to benefit from increased re-use of software and engineering knowledge across multiple products. And would still allow them to buy specialist functions from different Arm semiconductor partners. The business model relies on the semiconductor vendors paying licence and royalty fees, with the OEMs pulling on the Arm technology for their own benefit.

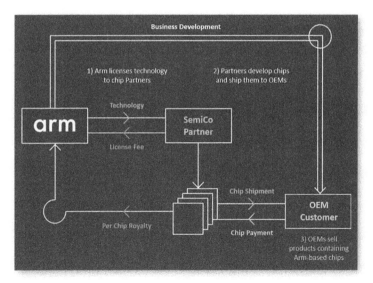

Arm's Business Model

The semiconductor partners get chip revenue using the processor IP, and everyone should benefit through lower costs and risk. The Arm strategy was to create OEM pull for the Arm processors: "Ask your semiconductor vendor to use an Arm processor, then you can re-use your knowledge and software assets across multiple projects." The strategy worked beautifully, especially as the cost and complexity of software have increased.

The number of markets requiring more advanced software has expanded significantly alongside consumers' increased expectations. These markets have benefited from the amortisation of costs available when using the Arm ecosystem. Being part of the Arm ecosystem of partners is good for business.

Software Tools

A microprocessor gains unparalleled flexibility from the ability to execute a set of instructions faithfully and quickly. Those instructions are binary codes that mean something to the microprocessor's digital logic, processor architects, and very few others. A sizable majority of software engineers may never see or care what the machine code looks like. These engineers will write their programs in a high-level language such as 'C', 'C++' or many other programming languages fit for different purposes. Software development tools provide the translation from these languages into the machine code understood by the processor.

The software development tools have some unique components (e.g. user interface) and some generic elements for each CPU type. The unique part is the core competence of the tools vendor, and users often become very attached to the way a particular tools package works: its visual interface and its features. Arm does not want to stand in the way of this market choice. So, Arm's mission has been to create a partnership of tools vendors that can target Arm's IP alongside developing and selling Arm's own tools.

As well as providing Arm's own unique set of development tool capabilities, Arm is regularly introducing new features into the processor architecture. These new features require tool enhancements, and few third-party vendors will want to invest in these changes until silicon is available. Arm's lead partners, however, need tools to support the new features while the IP and their SoCs are still in development. Arm, therefore, must always be the first to market with a complete set of software development tools for a new feature.

I believe Arm has managed to strike the right balance here: a vibrant third-party tools community supporting a processor architecture is a powerful strategy to create pull for Arm-based products. This choice is crucial in the microcontroller market, where the quality of the tools available often drives chip decisions. Arm's investment in software tools is essential but limited – we also want space for the third parties to succeed commercially.

Operating Systems

An operating system (OS) is the backbone on which computer systems are usually built. An OS interfaces to the low-level hardware, and provides services for the 'user' programs and rules under which they must operate. For a client device like a phone or laptop, the OS is the visible face of the product, e.g. iOS for Apple, Windows for a PC, or Android OS for many phones. The OS can play an equally important but more hidden role for servers and deeply embedded devices.

RTOS Program

In the case of deeply embedded devices, such as engine controllers for automotive or disc drive controllers, the operating systems are known as Real-Time Operating Systems (RTOSs). Porting an RTOS to different processor architectures can be challenging, requiring a lot of development and testing. Some markets are only accessible to processor architectures supported by key operating systems. However, an RTOS vendor is unlikely to port to a new architecture unless there are sufficient sales opportunities and existing silicon. Enabling ARM's semiconductor partners to win in those markets needed intervention.

The first move by ARM was in the mid-90s with the creation of the RTOS program. An ARM partner agreed to become a member of the program for a fee for access to an agreed list of RTOSs ported to the ARM architecture. ARM then funded the porting of the RTOSs, thus lowering the costs for each of the members and ensuring quality. Additional members also allowed the addition of new RTOSs. By the end of 1998, the number of RTOS program participants had grown to 14 (ARM, Annual Report, 1998). A clear benefit of being part of the ARM partnership.

Microsoft Windows CE Consortium

In November 1996, at the COMDEX expo, Microsoft announced the launch of Windows CE, a version of their popular PC operating system targeting embedded applications. Unfortunately for the ARM partnership, the first processors supported were only SH3, MIPS 3000 or MIPS 4000 (WindowsCE, 1996). ARM partners were reportedly being asked for considerable fees for a port, and so again, ARM stepped in and created the Windows CE Consortium. The consortium members effectively co-funded the port to the ARM architecture. By September 1997, version 2.0 of Windows CE also supported the ARM architecture – and by the end of 1998, there were five partners in the Windows CE Consortium (ARM, Annual Report, 1998). This diversity of ARM partners proved pivotal in the future development of this OS.

Other PDA OSs

The Pocket PC 2000 version from Microsoft, targeting Personal Digital Assistant (PDA) applications, was becoming popular, and the best-selling model series was Compaq's iPAQ using Digital Equipment's StrongARM processor. However, the market leader for PDA devices, Palm, Inc., used the Motorola Dragonball processor (Palm, 2002). In 2002, they released their Tungsten series running the latest Palm OS 5.0, which had now been ported to run on the ARM architecture. Again, the motivation was surely the availability of multiple ARM-based SoCs. The Tungsten T, for example, used the Texas Instruments OMAP processor (Tungsten, 2002).

In March 2002, Research in Motion (RIM) announced it was adding mobile phone capability to its popular Blackberry platform with its push email for corporations. The device used an ARM-based Qualcomm chipset, and later, RIM continued to keep their Blackberry OS focused on the ARM architecture with their first true smartphone, the Blackberry Bold series (RIM, 2011).

Symbian OS

A non-US operating system thread was underway in parallel. Psion of the UK had developed a 32-bit version of EPOC OS to support their new Psion Series 5 ARM-based PDA released in 1997 (PCW, 1997). Although the Series 5 was not the commercial success they wanted it to be, the 32-bit EPOC OS caught the attention of the major mobile phone players of the era. In June 1998, Symbian Ltd. was founded by Psion in conjunction with Nokia, Ericsson, and Motorola (Symbian, 1998) – with Matsushita, Siemens, and Samsung joining later. The Symbian OS was the basis for many future smartphones and, by 2007, powered around 125 million mobile phones a year – all with ARM-based CPUs. This ecosystem success had its roots in the ARM7100™ SoC we had built for Psion and their planned Series 5 PDA back in 1996.

Apple iPhone and Android OS Hit the Market

By 2007, all the major operating systems for mobile devices had been ported to run on the ARM architecture, and the ARM partnership was supplying >90% of the silicon volume. A resounding success for the partnership model. That year, a significant bombshell hit the market when Apple released the first iPhone in June, with iOS supporting downloadable Apps running on ARM-based CPU silicon. Suddenly the iPhone was the must-have smartphone, with the Symbian-based alternatives looking a bit dated. Crucially, Apple had provided the iPhone with a massive improvement in mobile web-browsing capability. Google, too, could see how the future of search would become more mobile-focused and moved very fast. By the end of the same year, their new Linux kernel and open source software-based Android OS were launched on the first phone by HTC (OHA, 2007). Although open source and available to port to any processor architecture, all the early commercial Android OS implementations were ARM architecture-based. By the time Intel was selling its first x86 Atom-based devices into the mobile phone market soon after, they had to fight the reality that the Android App stores were all ARM architecture optimised.

The Arm partners have seen unprecedented success in the mobile phone market, with more than one billion mobile phones shipped each year by 2020, enabled by the massive benefit of the operating systems being optimised to run on the Arm architecture.

Open Source Software

In the very early development of electronic computers, most software was written by academics and researchers working in collaboration – the default manner of working was to freely share the software to allow corrections and improvements (von Hippel & von Krogh, 2009). This early free and open sharing of the software declined as the software's complexity and perceived value started to increase. Commercial organisations wanted to monetise their considerable investments. Many of the previous section's examples are organisations creating commercial value from their OS products. Sharing the source code would be tantamount to giving the crown jewels away. In 1983, Richard Stallman launched the GNU Project and, soon after, the Free Software Foundation (open-source, 2022) – his mission was to create software free from constraints on the source code. Likeminded people joined the project, leading to the development of many sub-projects and activities. By the late 1990s, the term 'open source' was increasingly being used instead of 'free software' to acknowledge commercial opportunities of the software, too.

The GNU Project has created many tools for the community, including the well-known GNU C Compiler (GCC). However, it lacked a kernel operating system for a long time. In 1991, Linus Torvalds put this right by creating the Linux kernel on his PC, which was free from any commercial code, and in early 1992 released version 0.12 with the GNU General Public Licence (Linux, 1992). The combination of GNU and Linux now gave the open source community a readily available platform (the home PC) and a rapidly growing set of open source tools to play with. And they did. Many community members actively disliked Microsoft and the Windows world, so building an 'alternative' operating system and environment was part of the motivation. Others built complete desktop environments on top of these, such as the X Window System, and complete distributions appeared like Debian and Ubuntu.

It is possible to join the dots to see how the commercial OS vendors' interests and ARM's overlap, but it is harder to see how open source activities like GNU/Linux and ARM could create a situation of shared purpose and success. The PC heritage of Linux meant that it was focused on the x86 architecture initially. The open source nature of the project allowed others to port to new architectures, but most independent developers used a PC as their platform. Fortunately, ARM's legion of silicon partners was motivated to ensure Linux was ported to the ARM architecture. By 2006, there were very broadly three main uses of Linux: numerous ports onto embedded and mobile systems with the ARM architecture; PC-based distributions used by enthusiasts; and server systems either on Intel/HP's Itanium or Intel/AMD's x86.

In terms of system dollars, the server market was the biggest, but the embedded/mobile ARM market was by far the largest in terms of volume. So, although more commercial products shipped with Linux on ARM than any other architecture, most of the mainline developers and gatekeepers were x86 biased. ARM was actively engaged with the open source community and individual gatekeepers to push ARM architecture support back to the mainline. However, it was somewhat uncoordinated, with different ARM partners sometimes attempting to do the same with their ports. If there was to be an alignment of motivations between ARM and the open source community, things had to change.

The first change came about in 2007 with the dramatic entrance of Apple into the smartphone market and the industry realisation that mobile devices were becoming increasingly used to access the internet. Google's sponsorship of Android built on Linux for mobile devices led to a very rapid requirement to align more of the ARM open source activities. ARM then increased its investment in open source activities and, specifically, its engagement with the mainline developers.

Linaro

ARM wanted to do even more and needed a way to pool the partnership's resources and provide a single source of ARM architecture updates back to the mainline maintainers. By 2010 ARM had created Linaro in collaboration with many industry players (LWN, 2010). To quote from their site: "providing the tools, Linux kernel quality and security needed for a solid foundation to innovate on. Linaro works with member companies and the open source community to maintain the Arm software ecosystem and enable new markets on Arm architecture."

The next significant step forward was the public release of the Armv8 architecture supporting 64-bit addressing

(AARCH64) – a necessity for most server applications. With the very public message that ARM was targeting growth in the server market and the rapid increase in the number of ARM platforms available for development, the balance shifted to a more neutral stance among the Linux kernel developers and many of the other open source projects.

The ARM architecture was starting to be seen as a significant friend and sponsor to the open source activities. The Linaro activity provided a single ARM approved conduit to ensure the best ARM optimised code could be passed to the mainline developers. ARM now had the model of shared success desired where the actions of ARM, its partners, and independent developers alike could be aligned.

Electronic Design Automation (EDA)

With the relentless increase in transistor density provided by the semiconductor manufacturing process improvements, the number and size of the functions integrated into chips grow exponentially. Without the increasing sophistication of the EDA tools to design and verify the chips, the task would become uneconomic at least and impossible at worst. The EDA tools industry is one of the lynchpins of the semiconductor design community – the popularity of the Design Automation Conference (DAC) held annually is a testament to that.

The silicon partners need to use the EDA tools to integrate the Arm IP with their IP – so Arm's IP must work well with the EDA tools. And the converse is also true – the EDA vendors want to ensure their tools work well with the popular silicon IP of the day. The EDA vendors and Arm sell to the same customers, the semiconductor vendors, so it was natural that we formed very close relationships. However, we also had to acknowledge areas where we competed with IP and took great care to separate these activities.

The opportunity for mutual benefit is high, both for technical collaboration and marketing activities in many technology areas. Arm's culture of collaboration pre-disposed us to looking for these opportunities, too. We have had long and fruitful partnerships with the major EDA vendors and also many smaller vendors. The most complete activities were reference methodologies. These demonstrate how to get the best results when implementing Arm's processor IP from high-level language to fully place and routed designs using Arm's physical IP. The reference methodologies lowered the barriers to using Arm's IP and allowed the EDA vendors to demonstrate the capability of their tools. These activities really did result in shared success.

Words of Warning

Arm's collaboration and partnership culture was almost certainly used against it over the years. For example, Arm used to invite some third party vendors to the Arm Partners' Meeting, held annually. The purpose of those gatherings was to communicate with the partnership and for third-party vendors to demonstrate their support for the Arm technology. However, it's likely that Arm's openness with information on its roadmap of tools products, for example, stepped too far. We were probably enabling third parties to compete against us much more effectively by showing our plans.

At other times, our desire to partner with semiconductor vendors was not reciprocated as we would have desired. We might share internal project details to enable better collaboration, only for that information to be treated as a sign of weakness. Our intentions were to achieve a common goal, for example, the release of the partner's SoC. These situations were always tricky to navigate, but we believe defaulting to a partnership model was best overall for the business.

Chapter Summary and Lessons

The world of the ARM "partnership" in 1998 was focused on semiconductor companies; however, by 2015, the partnership had broadened to include EDA and software vendors, and many other third-party organisations. Each adding to the richness of support for the ARM architecture.

The chart below was used as a marketing tool, and, of course, the bigger, the better, it seemed. However, while it can be questioned just how invested some of the organisations were in the ARM architecture, what can't be in doubt is that if you wanted to develop an end-product using the ARM architecture, you would be entering an extremely rich and vibrant ecosystem.

The ARM "Connected Community" of 2015

What lessons can we learn from this?

1) **Share the benefits**. Keep in mind the benefits for partners, not just your own. How can you create a clear situation of sharing in success? – where their business interests align with your own selfish interests.

2) **Don't pick winners**. Of course, some partners will be more dynamic and successful than others, but take great care to give all the same opportunities. The word 'exclusive' was a nearly banned concept for Arm – instead, we offered a temporal advantage in early engagements with lead partners.

3) **Work with the community**. Where the commercial benefits are different, then take care to play carefully. For open source, Arm needed to work alongside their preferred ways of working and create shared success differently.

4) **Stoke demand**. Volumes matter in the chip business. Arm's partnership strategy worked because it incentivised success for everyone. Arm worked closely with OEMs to sell the value of the Arm ecosystem and create pull for the silicon partners. Third parties became interested when they could see a clear benefit of engaging with the Arm architecture. Success bred success.

Eight: Challenge Complacency

The day of the Initial Public Offering (IPO) of shares on 17th April 1998 was exciting. Would the market buy into ARM's future with confidence, or would it be a disappointment? The offer price was £5.75 on the LSE (before an eventual 20 to 1 split of the shares). By September 1998, the price was above £8. In the first five years of profitable growth, revenue had grown from £2.5m in 1993 to £42m in 1998 (~75% CAGR). Those were exceptional years. However, the market would be looking for something exceptional. Some in ARM feared whether it could continue to grow at the rate the market expected. While the business had created some excellent momentum with an increasing number of semiconductor partners in multiple regions, meaningful royalties were still a distant dream. The near-term revenue growth would need to come from increased licensing, tools, and services for several years to come.

Fortunately, the leadership team had not looked at the IPO as the end of the road, merely as a stepping stone – it wasn't in ARM's nature to sit back to enjoy the fruits of the IPO. Most of us believed there was a long, challenging journey ahead to meaningful royalties and market share. We still felt like underdogs in the market, fighting against other emerging IP players and many in-house CPUs. The competition in the embedded market had also intensified as ARM's success increased. The job was still far from complete.

ARM also faced a further self-inflicted challenge: quarterly scrutiny of ARM's company performance by the market investors. Without fail, ARM had to publicly report a healthy set of revenue, cost, and profit numbers every quarter. We needed to demonstrate growth in licences sold, licensing revenue, and numbers of royalty-bearing chips shipped while keeping costs acceptable. This challenge called for a level of discipline and predictability that ARM had been building toward for 2-3 years. Still, there's nothing like releasing information to the public every quarter to hone your skills.

Having a public share offering is most start-ups' dream: 'job done' for the initial investors. For ARM, the IPO was merely the first big step towards much bigger things. With many employees enjoying some early fruits of success after the IPO, how does a company ensure complacency doesn't set in? ARM tackled this danger directly and ambitiously with a combination of tools that kept the momentum high and ensured that any feelings of "we're there now" were quickly challenged and dispelled. As the revenue and number of colleagues grew, these tools became even more critical to the ongoing vitality of the organisation.

The Big, Scary Long-Term Goals

The book *Built to Last* (Collins & Porras, 2004) talks of Stimulating Progress with "Big Hairy Audacious Goals" (BHAGs) – the concept being to challenge an organisation beyond what might seem possible today. After the IPO, many of us had our first exposure to this mindset. ARM's leadership team knew that pursuing growth with our current tools wasn't enough. The organisation needed to think bigger, so that year, we embarked on a strategic planning exercise called 10x03 (ten times revenue by 2003).

10x03

Such strategy planning activities are nothing unusual, and all well-run companies would perform these. ARM had a particular challenge in 1998, though, addressing the expectations of the stock market and challenging any sense of complacency that may have taken hold. ARM's leadership team ensured the 10x03 activity wasn't confined to a small strategy team – it involved most of the company's senior staff. The leadership team believed there was tremendous knowledge deep in the organisation that needed to be heard (Urquhart, 2021). It was the first such strategic planning exercise that many of the non-founders had seen, and it was taken very seriously. The positive impact of the 10x03 activity was two-fold:

1 – ARM identified new activities that needed early investment if they were to yield results in the coming years. The most important of which was software. ARM needed to invest more in software development to support its partners' use of ARM's IP and to build new IP. Our mindset had been one of a hardware company, with software development tools being the only nod towards the software needs of end-products. That needed to change.

2 – We were all left in no doubt about the company's future ambitions. We knew ARM was good at microprocessor IP licensing, but ARM needed more – being good at this was vital but insufficient.

As an exercise in challenging complacency throughout the organisation, 10x03 served its purpose. ARM had successfully graduated from being a start-up, had achieved impressive growth, and the share price was looking good. The 10x03 planning activity told us more work was required to achieve ARM's goal of being a global RISC standard – the partners were shipping barely over 50m units a year, and royalty was less than 10% of overall revenue.

False Summits

The highest peak in England is Scafell Pike, and one of the popular routes is from Great Langdale (Wainwright, 1960) – a decent hike but very doable for the fit novice. One of the unfortunate features of this route, though, is that time and time again, it appears that the summit is in sight, only to find there's another summit beyond. You brace yourself for the next challenge, expecting it to be your last (and time for lunch), only to find there's more to do. Like trekking up Scafell Pike, every time ARM thought it had climbed to a pinnacle, we soon discovered, on further surveying, just how much more there was to do.

By the end of 2002, despite the historically bad semiconductor industry of the year before, ARM's partners shipped over 450m ARM-powered chips – a 9x improvement on four years previously (ARM, Annual Report, 2002). ARM could be forgiven for believing that their market-leading position for 32-bit processors by volume (Turley, 2002) meant we had already become the 'global RISC standard'. However, further investigation showed how big the opportunity was for the ARM processor in other markets – for example, the microcontroller market, which shipped billions of devices a year.

> "Every time ARM thought it had climbed to a pinnacle, we soon found... just how much more there was to do"

By the end of 2006, with the ARM partners shipping 2.4bn devices a year, you would again be forgiven for assuming there was no more market growth to be had. Yet the smartphone and tablet markets were yet to take off – these devices would lead to a tremendous surge in the functionality required per device. The dollar value of the chips would increase as performance and graphics expectations increased. And the number of additional functions would climb as new features such as Wi-Fi, Bluetooth, more advanced touch screens, and RFID were introduced. Each potentially requiring separate microprocessor-based chips. The big, hairy, audacious goal of 2007 was to become the number one architecture across all markets. This goal would require a simultaneous effort on multiple fronts: the very low-end microcontrollers, a big push for further energy efficiency in the mobile market, and a move to even higher performance products to support ARM in server applications.

By the time of the public launch of the first 64-bit capable architecture in 2011, ARM's partners were shipping nearly eight billion chips a year; and they still had a negligible share of the 'laptop' and server markets. And so, each false peak was followed by another as possibilities were opened up, new challenges understood, and ARM's partners' opportunities expanded.

The 'false summits' methodology worked exceptionally well to stimulate progress and challenge complacency.

Budgeting... Yawn

Everyone hates budgeting. Even those who claim to enjoy it don't really. You spend what feels like days pulling together information into spreadsheets to attempt to produce something you can justify and reason over. Then you get told the answer: The board have allocated you this revenue target and that cost budget for next year. The first is too high; the second is too low. Why did you bother producing something that could be explained?

I know it doesn't always happen like this; sometimes, you don't even need to do the first step – just wait for your budget to be given to you. My apologies for the cynicism, but hopefully, this illustrates a point. The annual budgeting process is often greeted with little enthusiasm and a fair amount of scepticism. This is a shame and can lead to missing out on one of the most critical elements of a great budget process.

In an ideal world, the annual budget process would be much more than producing a set of financial tables. The budget would be a narrative describing what the department or business intended to do the following year. What projects and activities would continue? What activities would cease? Perhaps, most importantly, what changes were needed to drive additional revenue or improve efficiency and effectiveness? It would, therefore, include deliberate plans to challenge and change the existing ways of running the business.

The long-term nature of ARM's business dictated that it was much more instructive to create rolling five-year plans. These gave the opportunity to include the costs and revenue associated with a roadmap of developments far more effectively and helped guide the expected growth rate of the business year to year.

It would be wrong to claim ARM got this right all the time, but we made a good attempt at this. The expected growth of the business demanded that ARM find new ways to build products and new markets to sell to. ARM's organisation was under continuous stress to evolve and do things better. There was the constant fear of getting left behind in technology stakes, not providing the performance or features that ARM's customers required, and not breaking into new markets at the expected rate of progress.

In short, the budgeting process was an ideal opportunity to drive change and ensure we had the most effective organisation and resources. Yes, ultimately, we did end up with a spreadsheet and, yes, more often than not, the numbers we finished with bore little resemblance to the initial requests. But the process of stretching and challenging was worthwhile to stimulate action.

The Quarterly Cycle

During the period 1998 to 2016, while ARM Holdings plc was listed on LSE and Nasdaq, very few people in the company would have been insulated from the quarterly pressures of delivering. Those in the sales organisation were tasked with facilitating the closure of contracts and were incentivised with bookings targets. For each region, each sales team needed to hit their bookings targets for each type of product. The future pipeline of revenue was a key metric for the business.

Engineering teams would need to deliver products to an agreed quality level so that ARM could start recognising revenue on new products. The engineers involved would undoubtedly have known the importance of their work to the quarter's revenue target.

The pressure was, at times, immense – the quarter Q3'2001 was particularly memorable, where a confluence of factors made it particularly tricky. The ARM926EJ-S™ was the hot new ticket for mobile with the Jazelle® feature to accelerate Java code execution and a general performance boost that partners needed. ARM had sold multiple new licences but was still developing the core. Unfortunately, revenue recognition rules changed regarding contemporaneous contracts that quarter, too. By 30th September 2001, the CPU engineering team needed to deliver the first revision of ARM926EJ-S to multiple partners for ARM to recognise about 80% of the licence revenue for the quarter. I can assure you the engineers felt very connected to the business that quarter. Yes, they did deliver – by the superhuman efforts of many involved.

With so many sources of revenue with different dependencies, closing a quarter was a tense time for sales, legal, licensing, and many in engineering. The operating machine at ARM worked extremely effectively over many, many quarters and years. It owed much to the excellent and open communication between different groups and people across all the continents. It was indeed an international collaboration and certainly ensured there was no room for complacency.

Product Roadmaps and Mid-Term Planning

Finalising product roadmaps was very difficult. Understandably there were many stakeholders. Partners invariably wanted better and sooner, engineering wanted more resources and time, and marketing wanted more features and new concepts to entice partners to reveal their needs. Due to the fast-moving nature of the industry, updating the roadmaps once a year was never enough, so ARM settled on the discipline of two per year. One aligned with the annual budget outcome, and one aligned with the ARM Partners' Meeting (APM, see next section) in August each year.

So what? Many companies do this. The most important lesson from ARM's experiences is that having the annual APM acted as the critical driver to force convergence between Engineering and Marketing on the one hand and between ARM and its partners on the other. We were all under continuous pressure to create new concepts, test them out, and evolve further. With consumer markets (Smartphones, Digital TVs, etc.) moving faster and faster each year, the speed of evolution for ARM's IP increased significantly, too.

I will now describe two activities related to roadmaps that demonstrated the spirit of ARM.

Mid-Term Planning

ARM ran a quarterly mid-term planning (MTP) process across all the engineering groups. The engineering leads' role was to plan the quarterly use of their resources for the next six quarters – to do this, they had to understand all the current commitments and all the likely new activities and developments. The discipline was to ensure the roadmaps for each product group were backed up by the MTP of available and future resources. Roadmaps could not be released to customers until there was a mutual agreement between Product Marketing and Engineering Management. Engineering was so well connected to the business goals and customers' needs that rarely did caution win. Roadmaps were always a stretch, but our best guess on what was possible with the planned resources. The process forced and built a strong partnership between the different disciplines.

Roadmaps Review

The second activity ensured ARM had alignment and partnership between product groups. Once a quarter, ARM ran the 'Roadmaps Review' to coincide with the roadmaps and the MTP updates. ARM's then CTO, Mike Muller, would act as the ultimate arbiter, demanding changes where needed. The goal was to have a cohesive set of product roadmaps. If a new architectural feature was to appear in a new processor in 12 months' time, then ARM needed to ensure that feature was supported first in the software tools and system IP, then all other related products. ARM's partners wouldn't care which business unit or division was developing a product – from their perspective, they were buying from ARM, not the separate groups. The software development tools needed to support new CPU features well before release to ensure ARM could develop software for the core. The Systems IP components were needed to support improved performance and features of the processors and had to be available on the same timeframes. The physical IP needed to be available for the target process technology, and so on. These events were highly effective in driving alignment across the organisation and removing any opportunity for complacency.

The Arm Partners' Meeting (APM)

Another significant source of activity that helped to stimulate progress was the annual APM. This meeting had been a yearly event since 1991 when the first meeting (then called the Technical Advisory Board) took place with 11 people in the boardroom of the barn.

The first Technical Advisory Board, 1991 (later APM)

Representatives of Acorn, Apple, and VLSI Technology met to discuss the technical roadmap of Advanced RISC Machines in the barn, Swaffham Bulbeck. It was part of the initial investment contract to ensure ARM embarked on good technical consultation with these partners. It was a great precedent that ARM extended to the new licensing partners and selected third parties from then on. Soon it would never be possible to get all the partners together around a single table again – a sure sign of progress. One of the ongoing challenges was whether to invite key technical managers or marketing people of ARM's partners. Mike Muller once told me that when we had technical people in the meetings, they wanted to talk about marketing and when we had marketing people, they wanted to talk about technology!

For many years ARM held the meetings during August at St John's College, University of Cambridge, before switching to Clare College. The partners were treated to a BBQ with a jazz band and an opportunity to be punted past the famous colleges along the River Cam.

2004 APM at St John's College, Cambridge

In contrast to the 1991 Technical Advisory Board meeting, there were 750 partners and 500 ARM employees at the 2004

APM. The meetings were a spectacular success, always oversubscribed and growing every year. It wasn't all about jazz bands and punting. Every day started at 9am with keynote presentations from the senior execs, followed by presentations and roadmaps from the product groups and segment marketing. The afternoons were filled with meetings between partners and ARM representatives. Every 30 minutes from 1pm to 6pm or beyond, ARM colleagues or partners would stand up in non-airconditioned meeting rooms, rush downstairs, across lawns, and up stairwells, to start another meeting. This was business speed-dating for three days in a row.

The APMs were the most important forcing function for prioritisation and stretch across the entire product development organisation. Starting in March every year, a dedicated team would attempt to agree on the major themes to present to the partners, and the product groups had to start updating their product roadmaps so that slides could be finalised by the end of June.

ARM's product roadmaps evolved a unique style, with different coloured symbols representing concept products, products in planning, those in development, and those ready to be delivered. They affectionately became known as roadmap "blobs". By using the same style year after year, ARM's long-term partners came to know and understand what was meant by a yellow blob or a blue one. The APMs were as necessary for the teams inside ARM's partners as they were for us. A chance for them to renew and create key relationships across ARM's organisation, learn of ARM's refreshed product roadmaps, and get a clear view of where the industry was headed. If ARM had its roadmaps right, we hoped to hear, "We want that, but sooner."

Chapter Summary and Lessons

A company's outside view will always be quite different from an inside view. Like a swan gliding along the water surface, with feet paddling at a breakneck speed below the surface, so Arm felt most of the time. Arm used many tools to keep complacency at bay. Some were our own making, but most were by ensuring the partners' needs were at the forefront of Arm's activities. Complacency was never an option by design:

1. **The summit is never reached**. Every time a breakthrough is made which leads to new business, treat it as an opportunity to horizon scan looking for the following peaks. Make those the next must-achieve goals for the organisation.

2. **Regular milestones.** Create a yearly calendar of operational milestones to ensure regular review and planning for the businesses.

3. **Force the pace**. Use internal operations and external customer events to demand pace from the organisation. Ensure standards are set high, and people are judged against achieving progress.

4. **No insulation**. Keep the organisation in touch with the reality of what is needed to deliver for each quarter. Not to scare people, but to energise them. Communicate and celebrate the successes of teamwork, like ARM926EJ-S delivery in Q3'01.

5. **Keep the team refreshed**. If there are signs of complacency, it needs intervention. Do people need new roles, is new blood required? Ensure the team always has a hunger for more.

Nine: Deal with Threats... Fast

Citius – Altius – Fortius[39] was the motto adopted at the launch of the Olympic Movement (Olympics, 1894). Its purpose was to inspire a competitive spirit in sport and a desire to continuously improve as an athlete. Seb Coe[40], a double Olympic Gold medal-winning middle-distance runner, took the threat of his big rival Steve Ovett very seriously whilst he was an active athlete (Guardian, 2020). He tells the story that one Christmas Day, settling back to relax, he suddenly realised that Steve wouldn't be resting – so he set off for his second training run of the day. That's taking threats seriously.

Business competition can also drive a 'faster, higher, stronger' attitude, and the way Arm harnessed that competition has been one of its secrets of success. Arm took all threats seriously, both to the direct business and to that of its partners, and we moved quickly. Even when the competition was nascent, we ran rather than walked. We believed you'd need to do something extraordinary to overtake us.

From where did this culture come? And what were the drivers?

---

[39] Faster – Higher – Stronger
[40] officially, Baron Sebastian Coe and now President of the IAAF

Taking Threats Seriously

As some of the previous chapters have hopefully illustrated, Arm built an organisation that demanded progress; the success of Arm's partners required it, and there was no room for complacency. Arm had also created a culture of open and collaborative communication both internally and with its partners. From the beginning, Robin Saxby had determined that the voice of the global semiconductor companies and OEMs had to be brought right inside the organisation. The culture and the organisation were built with environmental sensitivity – we cared what people said. If a partner told us they were having difficulty selling against a competitive processor, we'd want to know what could be done to assist their marketing. If a competitor announced their performance was better than ours, we'd try to find a way to close the gap and overtake. We knew our partners' businesses depended on us working together to demonstrate that the Arm solution was best for that application.

That is not to say Arm jumped on everything with equal enthusiasm. Some level of pragmatism would apply: did it impact our long-term royalties, IP licensing alone, our tools only, etc.? And we had to take care to not undermine existing partner solutions but instead encourage migration to newer technology over time. The critical point is that Arm created an organisation where threats were amplified to ensure they were fully heard and understood as widely as possible. And Arm tried to run fast with solutions, not allowing small threats to become big problems.

A word of caution is appropriate, though. A balance had to be struck to ensure the critical competitive messages could be heard amongst the noise. If the threat of competition or loss of a design-win was used too frequently without some filtering, then important messages could be ignored. I believe Arm's culture of questioning and debate helped us navigate through the fogginess of information. These checks and balances were vital to ensure we took threats seriously when warranted, without the organisation tuning out the 'noise'.

> *"Threats were amplified to ensure they were fully heard and understood"*

Many industry developments could have upset Arm and knocked it off course had we not reacted quickly and effectively. This chapter describes some of these, which came from various angles.

Technology Competition

The heart of a computer system is the general-purpose processor, or Central Processing Unit (CPU). The Acorn RISC Machine of 1985 was designed to be such a general-purpose processor. One which could run, albeit with effort, almost any computer program you want to throw at it – limited only by its resources and the timeframe available. A general-purpose CPU is excellent at running 'if this then that' style programs – just what is needed to run the operating system and most programs at the heart of computer systems.

Complex systems with additional functionality can soon present challenges beyond the capability of the CPU alone. At this point, the system designer will consider adding dedicated, specialist hardware. From a CPU vendor's perspective, this is either a threat to the value of the microprocessor, an opportunity to give it more capability, or an opportunity to build and sell that specialist processor. For Arm, these evolving market requirements were part of an ever-changing environment that had to be navigated continuously with care and attention.

Digital Signal Processors (DSPs)

All CPUs can do arithmetic operations, but a CPU can soon run into its performance limits if you want to perform repeated calculations on a data set. All applications for computing exist on a spectrum of data processing needs: from those a standard CPU can manage easily, through the more intense requirements suited to a dedicated DSP, right up to the millions of specialist cores at the heart of a supercomputer calculating next week's weather forecast.

At the lower end of this spectrum, ARM felt the early competition – an application might require some general-purpose computing with some repeated high-speed calculations within a tight power budget. Solutions like the ARC or Tensilica processors offer designers the option to add specialist instructions to boost performance. It sometimes made ARM's approach of a fixed instruction set seem inflexible and uncompetitive for these applications.

ARM believed that the least risky solution was to include better DSP capability into the standard processors. The first step down this path came with the fast multiplier addition to

ARM7DMI™. Next were the 'E' DSP[41] instructions added to the ARMv5TE architecture used in the ARM9E-S™ and ARM10E™ CPU cores. Next, ARM added Single Instruction Multiple Data (SIMD) instructions into the ARMv6 architecture and ARM11™ processors, Neon™ enhanced SIMD into Armv7 and enhanced Neon to Armv8 (ARM, A-Profile Architectures, 2022). The current culmination of efforts to improve data processing performance can be seen in the choice of the Armv8.2-A SVE[42] compliant processor in the Fujitsu A64FX™ at the heart of the Fugaku supercomputer– the fastest in the world as of 28th June 2021 (TOP500, 2021). A far cry from ARM's initial competitive response to a need for more data processing capability.

ARM often considered having its own standalone DSP IP with data processing performance and power efficiency beyond a standalone CPU. There were many already on the market. Having a competitive edge would have been tricky and put ARM in competition with key semiconductor partners. ARM's first attempt in the late 90s was called Piccolo. Although it had some excellent technical innovations, it proved highly unpopular with critical partners, and the commercial benefits looked weak. It was a very rare occasion where ARM killed a product far into its development. During the ADAPT process of 2002, ARM decided to adopt a more neutral stance – the so-called 'Switzerland' approach towards these standalone DSPs. We concluded that the right strategy was to continue adding capability to the CPU cores, partner to ensure the

---

[41] The 'E' was an insiders' 'joke' as it was codenamed El Segundo – our second attempt after an earlier DSP co-processor called Piccolo, which we killed

[42] Scalable Vector Extensions

dedicated DSPs worked well in ARM's software environment, and acquire more specialised data processing capability instead. In 2003, ARM acquired Adelante Technologies, whose highly configurable product became the Arm® OptimoDE™ product. This product allowed partners to build power-efficient, dedicated data processing engines suitable for specialist applications, such as audio processors at extremely low power consumption, e.g. hearing aids and MP3 players.

Java Acceleration

Sun Microsystems released Java[43] in 1995, designed to allow application developers to write once and run anywhere (Java, 1995). By the late 1990s, it was the hot news of the day, "all" software would be written in Java. This situation is something that we observed very carefully. CPUs needed to be able to execute the compiled Java byte codes, which most did with the help of a software interpreter. However, we feared that ARM's processors could become a commodity – any processor which can run Java byte codes would do. ARM's solution was the Jazelle® DBX™ architecture extension, first added to the ARM9™ core (hence the 'J' in ARM926EJ-S™), which directly executed most byte codes with a software environment to deal with the less common ones.

This solution significantly reduced memory footprint and lowered execution times, making it substantially more suitable for mobile phone systems than pure software interpreters. As Java was "the next big thing", the ARM926EJ-S was exceptionally successful: ARM sold over 100 licences, and the

---

[43] a programming language

partners shipped over five billion units. And despite the early hype, Java didn't become the only programming game in town – most embedded systems and significant operating systems continued to use 'C' and its cousins. Once again, ARM's strategy of building a general-purpose CPU that was great at Java execution proved to be the right solution for the partnership, and another potential threat was neutralised.

Security extensions

The ADAPT strategy exercise of 2002 identified two major technology areas of interest for computing systems. The first was security. How can ARM processor systems provide better solutions where software and hardware security are needed? For example, Digital Rights Management (DRM), cryptography, and mobile phone payments.

The solution used in many contemporary systems was to add an additional security processor with separate memory sitting alongside the central processor. As the sophistication of the security applications grew, however, that separate processor would need more capability. It was both a threat and an opportunity for ARM.

All operating systems which allow user programs have memory management requirements to prevent one application from interfering with another's data. However, to achieve the security demanded by content owners and banks, more was needed from the processor: secure software that was not accessible from the primary operating system (so-called normal world). A root of trust had to be established with hardware isolation and the creation of a Trusted Execution Environment.

ARM's unique solution was an invention codenamed Carbon and branded Arm® TrustZone®. This security feature supported the hardware isolation needed to allow security software to operate from secure memory (TrustZone, 2022). TrustZone was first added to the ARMv6 architecture and introduced with the ARM1176JZ-S™ processor in 2003, and it allowed a significant reduction in system complexity versus separate security processors. Although it was a popular addition commercially, it was many years before consumers could take full advantage of the capability in a mobile phone for tap and pay, for example.

When ARM invented Carbon, security extensions for processors were viewed as a niche requirement and not for the mainstream. Fast forward to the present age, and cyber security is now front and centre of computer system design. The latest Armv9 from Arm includes the Arm Confidential Compute Architecture (CCA) to build upon the existing security features of the Arm architecture (Grisenthwaite, 2021).

Fabless and Foundry

Until the foundation of Taiwan Semiconductor Manufacturing Company, Limited (TSMC) in 1987, silicon manufacturing fabs were usually wholly owned by the big semiconductor companies, the so-called Integrated Device Manufacturers (IDMs). The IDMs dominated the semiconductor industry, selling silicon chips that they commissioned, designed, manufactured, tested, and distributed. The founding of TSMC marked a disaggregation of the industry where it was now possible to have chips manufactured by a 'foundry' (TSMC, 1987). At the time of Advanced RISC Machines foundation, all the large semiconductor companies were IDMs with entirely in-house manufacturing operations. Licensing IDMs was a simple business model for ARM: License the IP to the semiconductor partner who keeps the IP entirely in-house through to packaged silicon.

The arrival of TSMC and other Foundry players in the 1990s opened new possibilities. For example, a company could do the complete chip design, including integrating the IP, then send it off to TSMC or another Foundry for the manufacture, which would ship wafers back for dicing, packaging, testing, and sale. These so-called Fabless companies were often only producing one chip for one market niche. They couldn't imagine using CPU IP for more than that one design, and they didn't need access to the entire IP, just models of it. From their perspective, the Foundry might buy the licence rights and also pay the royalty. There were multiple challenges with this model for ARM. Firstly, ARM's pricing model was based on the value of the packaged chip sold into the market – foundries, however, sold wafers that needed further processing into packaged chips. Furthermore, if ARM were to only license the Foundry manufacturers, then there would be no connection with the system designers who realised the value of the IP and no opportunity to understand their market needs.

Responding to these challenges, ARM needed to create an entirely new licensing model: The Foundry program was born. ARM reached an agreement with the foundries to develop and validate hard macros of the ARM7TDMI® (initially) on chosen processes. Then these hard macros were offered as per-use licences to Fabless silicon partners to integrate into their designs. They only had access to functional and timing models of the ARM IP, and delivered their layout to the Foundry with a 'hole' ready for the ARM IP to be integrated before manufacture.

The Fabless company would take the wafers, process them to produce the saleable devices, and pay ARM a royalty for each device sold.

This model took a lot of work to create, both internally and externally, as it was challenging to the existing licensing business model. Ultimately it provided a low-risk route for a new class of much smaller silicon vendors into the market without devaluing the ARM IP. It also provided a stepping stone to multi-use licences if these companies were successful. The program also restricted access to the highly valuable transistor-level ARM IP to the Foundries, enabling ARM to engage with a new class of company, even where IP risks were higher. It was a very successful competitive market response, but one ARM could have missed.

Soon some of the companies using Foundry manufacturing were not so small – they would be like IDM licensees in every other respect. For example, Qualcomm is a mobile radio specialist and had no interest in becoming a semiconductor manufacturer. Qualcomm wanted to build chips to service its customers with radio solutions – so it chose to be a fabless company from the start and has since become one of the largest. The licensing model evolved again, so Qualcomm and companies like them are treated the same way as IDMs were back in the beginning. The only difference is that they choose to outsource the manufacture of the wafers.

Intellectual Property Competitors

You could be forgiven for thinking that Arm's market leadership and financial results were possible due to weak competition. However, Arm has had to wrestle with plenty of solid competitors right from the start, and I believe this helped to spur Arm's success. For example, the MIPS Computer Systems' R3000 was a RISC processor available to license as an embedded microcell two years before the foundation of Advanced RISC Machines (R3000, 1988). The ARM founders constructed their strategy fully aware of this strong competitor and others. The challenge was to ensure the organisation stayed responsive to competitive threats as they arose.

This section will look at two competitive CPU IP vendors who significantly impacted Arm's consciousness and actions for different reasons. In most cases, I believe Arm felt that any threat could be tackled with better products and a determination that Arm could win in the long-term with a broader and deeper ecosystem. This defence was more successful in some markets than others.

MIPS Computer Systems, Inc.

MIPS Computer Systems, Inc. was founded in 1984 to commercialise the Reduced Instruction Set Computer (RISC) research undertaken by Dr John Hennessy at Stanford University (MIPS, 2022). MIPS' first product, released in 1986 as a chipset, was the R2000 with a 5-stage pipeline. Its RISC architecture gained a reputation for its performance and efficiency, leading to its use in workstation and server products. The R3000 of 1988 was a faster implementation, gained even more customers, and was sold as an embeddable microcell, too (R3000, 1988).

The R4000 of 1991 was one of the first 64-bit architecture processors, cementing MIPS' reputation for serving the high-end computer system market. ARM's contemporary product was a 3-stage pipelined, 32-bit microprocessor. It would be reasonable to surmise that ARM felt its current product sat in a performance space below the MIPS' products, with higher power efficiency. Although Apple had high hopes for the ARM610™, it was never intended to compete against the performance of the MIPS CPUs, which were almost always in larger, non-battery powered systems. ARM wished to develop higher performance products to follow the ARM610, but well before ARM got there, Silicon Graphics Computer Systems (SGI) acquired MIPS in 1992.

When Texas Instruments was bidding for the business at Nokia for the next-generation mobile device, SGI/MIPS was primarily focused on high-end CPUs intended for SGI's workstations. ARM won credibility for its small yet powerful RISC CPU suitable for the mobile application, while MIPS' gaze was elsewhere. The R8000 of 1994 and R10000 of 1996 demonstrate this high-end focus nicely. For years afterwards, the perception in many markets persisted of ARM products as low-end and MIPS as high-end.

In this period, ARM had been developing higher performance CPUs but within the power envelope of battery-powered devices. ARM released the ARM710™ in 1994, followed by the ARM810™ in 1996. The same year, Digital Semiconductor released the much higher-performance ARM instruction-set-compatible StrongARM processor (SA-110), which powered the final versions of the Apple Newton MessagePad. The StrongARM design came as a surprise to ARM initially. A team from Digital had looked at making a low-power processor and thought the ARM architecture might be an excellent place to start. So, they experimented and soon had an almost working ARM design. At this point, they came to tell us what they had done… without a licence. As befitted our collaborative nature and partnership model, ARM chose to embrace what they had done, and Digital became our first architectural licensee. From a competitive standpoint, this was an excellent decision. The SA-110 product created a wave of interest for its high performance and ability to remain within the requirements of a battery-operated device. That interest reflected very well on ARM solutions in general.

In embedded markets, ARM was now viewed as having high-performance solutions, too. The competitive pressure from the MIPS CPUs hadn't been felt as strongly as it could have been. With MIPS' product development within SGI, only companies such as LSI Logic and NEC Corporation continued to push the R3000 derivatives into embedded markets. This situation was about to change, but ARM was in a good position to react.

In 1998, MIPS Technologies, Inc. was spun out from SGI via another IPO with a more purposeful approach to licensing the core technology and embedded markets. Once again, it was a direct licensing competitor in the market. In the same year, ARM released the first of its ARM9 range of processors. Now, both ARM and MIPS were marketing licensable processors of similar performance for embedded markets. MIPS had its back-catalogue of higher performance cores to retrofit to embedded, while ARM was working its way up the performance curve. In handheld, battery-powered markets, ARM's design wins in mobile phones, and a growing list of partners ensured we were on the front foot. MIPS would have to work hard to overcome the ARM ecosystem and the perception of ARM's superior power efficiency. Each subsequent generation of phones added features and capabilities, so the mobile OEMs and their semiconductor suppliers demanded more performance from the CPU. To ensure these companies didn't switch to MIPS or other solutions, ARM increased its investment in CPU development to accelerate schedules. In parallel with the development of the ARM9 products in the Cambridge, UK office, in 1997, ARM opened a new CPU design centre in Austin, Texas. After Dave Jaggar's relocation, this group quickly grew under his leadership, delivering the ARM1020E™ of 2001.

While the Austin office completed the ARM10, the expanded Cambridge office worked on its successor. The ARM1136J-S™ was announced in 2002, offering approximately twice the performance of the ARM9 products. With the accelerating performance of ARM's CPUs (the Austin-designed Cortex®-A8™ of 2005 doubled performance again), the ARM partnership was winning nearly all the mobile phone and PDA sockets. With increased performance came the opportunity for ARM's CPUs to compete in non-mobile markets. Some of ARM's partners prioritised MIPS for higher performance markets, like Set Top Boxes (STB) and networking. The ARM1176JZ-S announced in 2003 offered a big performance leap on ARM9 and Java acceleration features that MIPS' cores lacked.

A performance battle was underway in non-mobile, where multiple software threads would run simultaneously. MIPS favoured adding multi threading capability to high-performance cores. At the same time, ARM thought that multiple, more efficient cores would be a better approach to achieve the necessary performance with better power efficiency. NEC (now Renesas) agreed, and it became the lead partner for the ARM11MPCore™ of 2004. This approach, called Symmetric

Multi-Processing (SMP), became the standard feature of all ARM's future application CPUs. ARM's traditional focus on power efficiency had proven the right path again.

Features such as Jazelle, SMP, and TrustZone, and the increasing performance – yet with power-efficiency – of the ARM CPU roadmap, enabled ARM's partners to win more and more sockets in markets that previously had needed the higher performance that MIPS and others offered. The ARM-based software ecosystem was growing, too, spilling over from handheld devices, leaving MIPS with fewer markets where they offered benefits versus ARM solutions.

In 2013, after some years of stagnant revenue, MIPS was bought by Imagination Technologies, then sold to a venture capital company in 2017, sold again in 2018, went bankrupt, and was finally resurrected in March 2021 as "MIPS" (MIPS, 2022). ARM took no pleasure in the demise of such a competent technical competitor. The MIPS processors had spurred ARM to develop many features and products to help its partners win new sockets. The competition had been very good for ARM.

ARC (now part of Synopsys Inc.)

ARC is the second example of an IP licensing competitor to illustrate ARM's threat management in action. Argonaut Games (a UK company) designed the original Argonaut RISC Core (ARC) for their internal use. By 1997, ARC International was formed to develop and promote the processor family to the broader industry. As well as being a highly efficient 32-bit RISC core, their unique selling proposition is the use of a processor configurator to allow a system designer to select functions and instructions on a modular basis. Furthermore, it is possible to add custom instructions, making it a very attractive proposition for some applications.

This reconfigurability has often been used as a competitive stick to beat ARM, usually where improved DSP capabilities are required. ARM's response had two elements. Firstly, ARM's premise has been the importance of risk reduction and time-to-market in SoC design. Many aspects can go wrong during the design process, so ARM thought it better to use CPU IP without instruction changes. ARM believed we could appeal to the business managers of SoC developments where risk reduction would resonate more.

Secondly, ARM's competitive response emphasised the importance of the software ecosystem: An "ARM is an ARM". So, ARM added increasing data processing capability to the architecture so that software development tools and software libraries could be proven on known, standard configurations of each processor in the market. A device containing a standard ARM processor such as Cortex-M4™ from one manufacturer would be identical to another's, allowing the same software functions to work precisely as intended. Most recently, Arm responded to the competitive pressure for better Machine Learning and DSP performance in the Cortex-M family with the addition of Arm® Helium™ technology in the Cortex-M55™.

ARC remains a strong competitor, especially in the hands of Synopsys, causing Arm to continually assess its threat response.

Key Take-Aways

There can be very few companies without direct competitors in a marketplace. ARM was not unique here. The culture and organisational response to this competition gave ARM an extra string to its bow. There was a hunger inside the organisation to understand the details whenever a design-win was lost. The network of segment marketing and partner managers would often ensure the full facts could be understood and assessed. The product marketing and engineering teams would debate whether there was an appropriate technical response. Most of all, ARM tried to catch emerging trends early to ensure we could quickly improve our competitiveness.

The Battle for Smartphones and Tablets

Taking a different direction now, this threat to ARM was caused by a semiconductor company using their proprietary CPU technology to attack the market leadership of the ARM ecosystem. It was common for an ARM partner to use their CPU technology in some markets. However, the situation with Intel in smartphone and tablet markets felt like a near-existential threat at the time. Intel has been the largest semiconductor company for many years, with a powerful consumer brand.

The highest performance processor in a modern phone is the so-called Applications processor, which runs the operating system and any 'Apps'. This CPU is felt to be the heart of the phone, drives the software ecosystem, and is usually the highest value silicon of a smartphone or tablet. Intel's direct attempt to win Applications processor sockets with their x86 architecture CPUs was a direct assault on ARM and its partners.

The earliest mobile phones were the size and shape of a brick with a large aerial. However, they were considerably smaller by the time they had become consumer devices, albeit with a tiny monochrome screen and a still chunky battery.

The advent of digital cellular phones was a turning point for the design of their electronics. Now microcontrollers were employed along with DSPs to convert your voice into the highly encoded signal broadcast over the radio (and the reverse process on reception). When Nokia chose to use a 32-bit ARM processor to sit next to the DSP, it was endowed with a lot more processing capability than needed for just making the phone calls. Those who owned a Nokia in the late 90s will remember the height of game complexity: Snake. A highly addictive game that worked on tiny screens and was the start of mobile time-wasting for millions.

As consumers started to want more and more functions on their phones, the screens grew bigger, had higher resolution, and became colour. The applications increased to include calendars, larger and better phone directories, better games, and, inevitably, web browsing and email. As consumers were able to do more with their phones, so they wanted to do even more, and market competition brought us to the smartphones of the early 2000s.

The first smartphone I used was the Sony-Ericsson P800 in 2004, which blew away my colleagues when I travelled to the US with an early version. A few years later, in 2007, they had reason to be equally smug – the launch of the Apple iPhone.

Intel's ARM-based XScale™

The processor requirements of these phones were rising rapidly along with consumers' expectations. This opportunity caught the attention of Intel Corporation, the inventor of the world's first microprocessor and the gorilla of the PC and laptop markets with their x86 architecture chips. In 1998, while settling a patent dispute, Intel acquired Digital Semiconductor's StrongARM design and chose to license the ARM architecture for use in mobile phones. Intel then created the PXA210 (XScale) processor following ARM's instruction-set-architecture blueprint. It planned to use its semiconductor manufacturing leadership to provide the market's highest performance ARM CPUs and win over as many sockets as possible to Intel.

This was a new, interesting dynamic for ARM to deal with – Intel was an ARM partner selling ARM-based cores. That's good. However, ARM also wanted other partners to have opportunities to sell to the same OEMs. As ARM's semiconductor partners could not use the Intel XScale, ARM responded with high performance, licensable cores to enable them: the ARM11 family, then Cortex-A8, Cortex-A9™ and beyond.

Intel only had one competitor of concern in the PC market, AMD, and they kept one step ahead to ensure they held 90% market share. However, in the mobile phone market, the competition from existing ARM partners was intense. They didn't have enough advantage, and OEMs weren't keen to give Intel the margins they had hoped for. Intel then started to build additional instruction features into XScale: Wireless MMX for improved multimedia performance in the PXA27x series of 2004 (Intel, 2004). This technology, they hoped, would give them the hook of differentiation and stickiness they needed. ARM feared this would lead to an imbalance of competition in the market and responded with the Neon multimedia extensions for Armv7, first implemented in Cortex-A8. It's probable that some of the OEMs in the mobile market also saw Intel's Wireless MMX as a threat to their purchasing flexibility. The mobile market was not the PC market – Intel was not going to dominate that easily.

Intel's Low Power x86: The Atom™

Another factor came into play, which probably pushed them to make a big decision. In 2002, when Intel entered the market with an ARM-based product, there was clear blue water between the relatively immature smartphone/PDA market and the Windows-powered laptop market. There was a clear differentiation of markets: the small screen, low functionality mobiles on the one hand, and the high performance, high functionality PC on the other. Using different processor architectures in each made some sense. However, by 2006, that functionality gap was shrinking. It was only a matter of time before high-end mobile devices with internet browsing capability would compete with laptops for the consumers' attention. Intel had decided that the path to significant revenue and profits in the mobile market was better served with a different strategy.

They sold their XScale business to Marvell in June 2006. For now, all seemed quiet on the Intel front – it looked to outsiders as if they had tried and failed in the mobile market.

When Intel returned to the market, it did so with a renewed, aggressive strategy to attack the ARM ecosystem. As the capability of the wireless networks improved along with the high-end mobiles, more and more users wished to access the internet. As Apple launched the iPhone in 2007 with one of the best mobile browser experiences available, most websites were still optimised for desktop computer screens and capabilities. Something had to change. In Intel's view, the processor was part of the problem (or solution, depending on your standpoint). They had decided to revert to using the x86 architecture to tackle the emerging smartphone and tablet markets. After the relative quiet of nearly two years, Intel announced the low-power x86: the Intel Atom™ processor family. The Atom, Intel believed, could compete with ARM's in the sub-2 Watt space, with access to a software ecosystem already available to provide the internet browsing capability users wanted.

The Race Was On

As soon as Intel switched horses to their own processor architecture, the dynamic for ARM and many in the industry changed significantly. They were now targeting ARM and its partnership; we were both in their crosshairs – their high-margin chip business of laptops and PCs was under threat, and we were the problem. Intel had considerable advantages with high-performance products, brand recognition, silicon process, high-end ecosystem, and finances[44]. It's hard to overestimate the enormity of the challenge that the ARM partnership appeared to have. Could it be that ARM's products would be restricted to lower-end platforms while Intel rode off with the high-end smartphone and newly emerging tablet markets?

ARM had not been standing still while Intel was producing XScale processors; the Cortex-A8 of 2005 and the multicore Cortex-A9 of 2008 were both very capable high-performance processors that multiple ARM partners licensed. Though designated a mobile core by Intel, the Intel Atom was still a relatively hot processor, consuming more than 1 Watt to the equivalent performance ARM processor's much less than 1 Watt. The ARM architecture appeared to have a significant power-efficiency advantage. The low power consumption of

---

[44] Linux servers, Intel Inside™, Intel revenue in 2006: $35.6B, ARM Limited revenue $483.6M

ARM-based chips allowed smaller batteries, less weighty heat sinks, and hence lower-cost products to be produced by OEMs. For now, at least, the Atom wasn't ready for smartphones.

The race was on. The ARM ecosystem needed to be enhanced to ensure the internet browsing experience on ARM was as good as that on a laptop. Intel needed to drive the Atom down to the suitable power consumption for smartphones.

ARM's business model pulled in cents per chip, Intel's tens to hundreds of dollars per chip. However, ARM had no choice but to take on this challenge – it was the single most potent unifying challenge the company could have possibly wished for. Thank you, Intel (easier to say in hindsight). This battle wasn't ARM's fight alone. Intel's ambitions were a severe threat to almost everyone in the ARM partnership's mobile phone ecosystem. Intel had effectively declared war on not just one competitor, as they had with AMD in the PC and server market, but with dozens of semiconductor companies using the ARM processor. And worse for Intel, each of these would compete with different specialities.

Intel's claim for switching to x86 was that smartphones were arriving on the market with an expectation of internet access and the ability to web-browse. In 2007, most websites were expecting clients based on x86 based platforms (PCs), and specific browser add-ons, particularly Adobe Flash™, were only available for x86. Using Fear, Uncertainty, and Doubt (FUD), Intel was marketing that the internet was made for x86 and that this was the only option for high-end client devices. Good marketing, but one ARM needed to take apart quickly. We had something to target directly when Intel published a list of 40 websites that worked on Intel x86 processors (PCs) but not on

ARM-based mobile browsers. ARM quickly discovered that it had natural allies, too. For example, Nokia was building a Linux-based tablet device that needed a good web browsing experience. Working with their contractor, we quickly established the technical causes. With a quick bit of environment porting to the ARM-based browser and an ARM port of Flash Player, all the websites in question started to work perfectly on the device. Soon afterwards, the ARM team demonstrated this at the 2007 ARM Developers' Conference. 1-1 draw so far. This engagement was just an early skirmish. However, ARM was emboldened – the claim that "the Internet runs on x86" was only skin deep, and the ARM partnership had rallied in response.

Open Source Software

There existed a middle ground between laptops and smartphones: Linux-based tablets. These products were the central place of battle. Whoever could move more quickly might win sockets here. Intel had an advantage – Linux had been developed on the PC, and most commercial use-cases were on x86, albeit at the server level. Nonetheless, there were many ports of Linux to ARM processors, but most were done independently and not folded back into the mainline.

ARM discovered, for example, that one of the major Linux distributions, Debian, did not support the ARM architecture, although it did the x86. On further investigation, it seemed that nobody had compiled the Fortran libraries on ARM, which is necessary to 'complete' the build. The fundamental problem was that the open source developers were used to working on x86 based PCs, and there were no consumer-available ARM-based software development platforms. Fortunately, by late 2007 some networked Hard Discs appeared on the market built with ARM-based silicon running Linux. These were easy to repurpose as ARM development systems. I was put in contact with an open source developer and promised to pay for his time if he'd get Debian working. Three days after posting one of these network drives, Debian was fully working on ARM – before we'd even raised a purchase order for him to do the work! This activity was a great example of working side-by-side with motivated open source developers.

This, though, was scratching the surface. ARM needed to accelerate the adoption rate of ARM architecture support in the Linux kernel and dozens of other open source projects. By 2010 ARM had created Linaro (LWN, 2010) in partnership with many industry players. ARM now had an open source organisation dedicated to the ARM architecture, which could start to compete with the Intel x86 machine. ARM had once again neutralised a perceived key ecosystem advantage of x86 processors.

Fusion and the End-Game (for now)

There is nothing like existential threats to bring people together – both inside ARM and across the partnership. In 2005 ARM had created business divisions and some smaller units, which ARM hoped would grow into more extensive business lines. As the threat of low power x86 became clearer, ARM needed to strengthen the CPU competitiveness and re-align more activities to support this. ARM moved the System IP business unit into the Processor Division to create better technical alignment, for example. Some in ARM believed that if we got the strategy right, it would not just prevent Intel from winning ARM's high-end business but also lead to more opportunities for the ARM partnership. Although ARM didn't formally call this the 'Fusion' project, this terminology was used in the strategy discussions. One consequence was the re-assertion of ARM's desire to be the number one CPU architecture across the entire industry, from sensors to servers – why stop at screen-based devices? ARM also needed to support the faster development of the high-performance roadmap while keeping ARM's competitive advantage in system power consumption. So low-power leadership became a rallying call, too.

ARM and the partnership wanted access to the highest performance manufacturing process technology, and ARM found willing allies among the foundries. They realised that the more chips in mobile that were Intel chips, the fewer wafers they would be manufacturing. ARM focused the physical IP efforts on ensuring partners could manufacture at foundries with the performance and power required to win at the high-end.

The foundries were an example of what ARM found in much of the semiconductor industry. Many third-party companies were healthy because dozens of semiconductor partners were fighting for business in mobile using the ARM architecture. Intel was a threat not only to ARM and its semiconductor partners but also to many third-party companies.

Intel did as they intended and built low-power products based on the x86 architecture for the mobile market. These devices became successively better suited to the smartphone and tablet markets. However, they found they needed to use market incentives to help vendors move away from the de facto standard of ARM (Reuters, 2014). The Android OS supported non-ARM architecture solutions, but the Google Apps store was all ARM-optimised. Intel created an incentive scheme to get

Apps writers to port over to x86 architecture. Everything that helped Intel hold onto the Windows PC market was working against it in the smartphone and tablet market, where the leading architecture was ARM.

Intel also had to overcome another significant challenge. The economic model of processor SoCs in the mobile market was significantly different from the one Intel experienced for PCs. A high-end processor in mobile might cost $15 in volume versus $40+ in a low-end laptop. To make a good enough return on investment, Intel would need to sell chips at a higher price than the market expected. Developing a microprocessor architecture, associated SoCs, and manufacturing processes is expensive. Your investment dollars need to be recouped with premium prices and significant volumes – precisely why the ARM licensing model worked so well for the partnership. ARM partners need only invest in the SoC development, buy a licence to the processor, and use a Foundry for the manufacturing. The return for Intel was hard to find.

When Apple was considering which processor to use for the iPhone, Intel was interested (Madrigal, 2013). However, the price Apple wanted to pay for the chip was lower than the manufacturing price Intel could achieve – so they passed and may have forever regretted it. Intel's manufacturing plants were optimised for high-performance processors in the PC and server markets with good margins. Higher volume, power-optimised parts would have required different manufacturing plants or external foundries.

Ultimately, an ecosystem of supplier-choice with an ARM optimised software ecosystem led to Intel's withdrawal from mobile in 2016 and a victory for the ARM partnership. It was quicker, lower cost, and more successful to build your phone based on the ARM processor architecture, and that's what the market did.

Chapter Summary and Lessons

There is no single way to deal with competition – every competitor and circumstance is different. The lessons to be learnt from Arm's relative success here are universally applicable, though.

1) **Be sensitive**. Set up systems that set off alarm bells whenever competitors win against you – make sure your business groups hear and understand why. Aim for an excellent understanding of the market and use the ecosystem as part of the antennae. Don't be tempted to brush the inconvenient truth to one side; don't shoot the messengers: learn.

2) **Threat or Opportunity**. Is this situation a threat to a product line or an opportunity to build a new one? Once a threat is better understood, turn it on its head and work out how to succeed in the new situation.

3) **Take action**. Create some energy for change, point the way and get going. Make the status quo unacceptable internally. Don't wait until the competition has gained chunks of the market before you act.

4) **Run, don't walk**. Deal with challenges while they are small. It's much easier and will pay back in multiples. Once a new strategy is agreed upon, move quickly, learn some more, and keep going… at pace.

Ten: Stay Unified

Of all the 'difficult steps' taken by Arm on its journey, staying unified as an organisation was one of the most challenging yet vital for achieving its goals. Increasing the shipments of royalty-bearing chips has been the primary tangible but non-financial objective since the earliest days of Advanced RISC Machines[45]. Of course, sustainable revenue and profit growth are any commercial organisation's ultimate aims. However, Arm's single non-financial objective has proven to provide the near-perfect hook on which to build Arm's increasingly diversified business. With the diversification of business lines and geographic spread of offices, tensions naturally grow between the local business goals and the desire to remain one-Arm. A reasonable question is: What are the benefits of staying unified as a business?

For Arm, there were at least two significant benefits. Firstly, as each business unit generates products and revenue, it enhances the Arm ecosystem's competitive position by deepening business opportunities for partners. Secondly, keeping a unified organisational culture drives a willingness of individuals to 'do the right thing' when presented with complex trade-offs. My experience was that people were far more willing to offer help and, importantly, to listen to ideas offered from outside their group when they felt part of one

---

[45] Later supplemented with increasing the value of IP on each chip

overall organisation. It created a shared purpose that energised people to work together, share ideas, and always look for ways to improve despite the challenges of their own goals.

Staying unified, therefore, was one of the most important goals for Arm as an organisation, and of all the 'difficult steps', it was one of the most challenging to maintain. Any well-run organisation's business strategy probably contains many elements of Arm's recipe for success. However, focusing on organisational culture, particularly a feeling of unity, requires a new level of deliberate action. In this chapter, I'll outline some of the measures taken to maintain this alignment and how Arm was able to use outside influences to assist, too.

The Challenges of Growth

Being in a start-up is often an exciting experience with a small number of founders who know each other well and have high motivation. If the early technology or commercial milestones are hit, then the sense of excitement and togetherness will grow and deepen. Then more people are hired, the business diversifies, and people start to go in their own directions with different goals and motivations. Suddenly that sense of camaraderie is harder to find. But is this inevitable?

Arm managed to hold onto a start-up feeling for a long time, but it wasn't easy. As Arm grew from 12 people to 50 to 200 to 1000 and beyond, we largely managed to retain that sense of fighting as one body. Arm managed to stay unified. It truly felt like a friendly, welcoming, and unified company for a long time beyond the start-up years and the IPO of 1998. I'm sure this wasn't universal, but it was true for many more people than might typically be expected. And this feeling of being part of one company, fighting for the same goals, extended not just between engineering groups but also between functional departments.

As with many great things about Arm, it all started with a strong foundation, and then a myriad of different elements came together to help maintain the feeling of unity as we grew.

One Company, One Goal

One of the most important consequences of the business model is its clear view of what long-term success requires: high volume manufacture of chips containing royalty-bearing IP. This clarity and simplicity strongly impacted our working culture and behaviours. Most people also understood that revenue now was not just a business goal in itself but a strong indicator of future potential royalties. Every IP licence, service contract, or software tool sold indicated investment by partners to build future royalty-bearing products. Revenue from all businesses mattered and acted as a great unifier.

For an engineer working in the group delivering CPU cores, the link from their work to this goal is clear and straightforward. However, what about people working in the other groups of Arm?

The beauty of this long-term goal is that the link from just about every part of the organisation was nearly as short and clear. If your role was to build the 'C' compiler, you knew that this was vital to ensure ARM's partners could write software for the end products. Similarly, an engineer working in the Application Engineering support group knew they were the essential glue that helped partners accelerate their design-in of the Arm technology. Each group had short-term financial targets, but every group knew that increasing the number of royalty-bearing chips sold was the end goal, and we all could share in the reflected glory of royalties.

This "One company, one goal" nature of Arm gave a powerful sense of camaraderie. We were on a mission together, and although we had different roles and priorities at any given time, there was a strong sense of togetherness that, 25 years after I joined, was still felt strongly.

Which Comes First?

The desire for unity or the unifying goal?

In the case of Arm, the goal of royalty-bearing chip shipments came first. Arm's early leaders created the strategy to achieve this encompassing goal, structured the organisation appropriately, and encouraged a unifying culture.

If unity is the need, then creating a single organisational goal should be the first step. The goal would need to be simple yet compelling, providing a clarity of purpose for the organisation. Validation of its effectiveness would be to ask: to what extent do the separate business groups or departments work towards the company goal while driving their own local goals?

This requirement may seem obvious through the lens of unity, but it's surprising how many organisations have lost sight of the power of unifying goals.

Other Benefits of Unity

For most people, it's just a nicer place to be. Knowing your work colleagues have shared goals or purpose should enable a more engaging work environment. It will lubricate social and business interactions and lead to greater levels of trust. In cold business terms, having a shared purpose makes it easier to collaborate with colleagues and encourages the right actions to maximise profit.

In my experience at Arm, staying unified led to a more collegiate feeling and better business outcomes. I'll describe two other significant benefits below.

Diversity and Inclusion

Many years after Arm's founding, the idea that diversity was necessary but insufficient has become a strong driver of business practice. Ensuring your organisation has a diversity of backgrounds and outlooks has been shown to be fair and a strong driver of business outcomes. There is an important 'but': only if you ensure everyone is able to contribute. Everybody must feel included and have a voice as valued as anyone else's. His experiences at Motorola drove Robin Saxby's strong motivation in this area (Saxby, 2021). Robin told of a particular training course on "synergy" where his overriding lesson was that the sum of the parts is greater than the parts, and that the quietest people in the room sometimes have the most valuable things to say. You get better synergy when you make a conscious effort to level up everyone's contribution (inclusivity).

It would be a stretch to say Arm did a perfect job of ensuring high diversity by modern standards in its early days. Still, it's worth noting that the first new employee after the foundation was a female engineer when far too few women were in the chip design industry in 1991. With a bit of boldness, I will say that there was little inherent bias towards people of different backgrounds – the main focus was on capability and potential. As a company with global ambitions, Arm had a naturally global view of people and their skills. Arm was, however, selecting from the pool of talent available – as non-diverse by modern standards as that may have been.

Overall, Arm is now a very diverse company with many national cultures and backgrounds. The international nature of the business, the royalty units' goal, and the need for cross-border cooperation favoured those who showed a curiosity for learning about other cultures. International travel was widespread and expected throughout Arm's journey, right up to the Covid-19 crisis of early 2020. Jet travel was not good for the environment or Arm's costs, but it played a crucial role in fostering an inclusive and well-connected culture. Travelling with colleagues, even just the taxi ride to Heathrow airport from Cambridge, was a great way to get to know people outside your group and those more senior to us.

Another consequence of the strong culture of inclusion was that Arm was very open with information and very 'chatty' – people loved to talk about everything in the kitchen or down the pub. And I mean everything: your project, my project, the other department, whether things were being done in the right way, the latest customer feedback, etc., etc. Arm built a strong culture of debate and discussion – that didn't mean decisions had to be agreed upon by everyone, although it may have felt like that for some people. Suppose you arrived from a company where the culture was to keep conversations within groups and for strong decision-makers. In that case, it was frustrating to find almost everything being questioned and challenged… even by people not in your function. Of course, this meant that some decisions did seem to take longer, but we believed, in most cases, that alignment was as impactful as the decision itself.

The fallout from this level of inclusivity and strong culture is that some people just didn't fit in. They wanted to keep information to themselves and resented being challenged "by people less informed or qualified than them" – the answer: get used to it and start to value the benefits, or leave and find a company where you won't be challenged. The rest of us learnt to thrive or survive in an environment where almost everything was open to being dissected and debated – determined to find a better way. The early leadership team of Advanced RISC Machines had chosen this path and expected to be challenged. It led to a culture where people joining learnt that speaking their mind, even to more senior people, was not just allowed but expected. Extending that culture across borders and to a much larger organisation was hard, but the "Big Picture" induction conferences, the international cooperation needed, and the one-company one-goal nature of Arm helped enormously.

Inclusion of people in the concerns of the business was part of what helped us stay unified as an organisation. And the flip side was that the desire for unity to achieve our shared purpose meant we wanted to create an organisation of inclusivity – another virtuous circle.

Helpfulness and Innovation

Arm has won many awards for Innovation, not that we ever felt good enough. In 2016, some colleagues and I were invited to present ARM's methods to encourage innovative behaviour to outside executives. There was some nodding of heads and applauding of what we had done, but then some reflected that they didn't see how they could emulate us. We were perplexed when they described the lack of sharing and communication across department or country borders. How can you possibly run an organisation without openness and a shared feeling of being one organisation?

Our culture, it seemed, ran deep. While we were pleased to receive those innovation awards and the occasional compliments, we didn't think we deserved it. All we were doing was working together, striving to meet our business goals and build better products. Wasn't this a necessity of being part of one organisation with one common goal?

Margaret Heffernan (Heffernan, 2014) helped us understand this better. She came and presented at one of our group planning events on innovation and explained that among the key drivers (such as diversity and inclusion), one of the most impactful was "helpfulness". Will people in your organisation go beyond their job description to help others achieve their goals? Will people in the sales team make time to get to know the design engineers to ensure they understand the customers' requirements? Will a verification engineer from one group seek out other verification engineers to share ideas and best practices? Will you share information openly when asked and welcome questions and challenges? It is being helpful, not intrusive.

If we all feel we are part of the 'gang', all aiming for the same goals, then going beyond your job description is natural and necessary. Going beyond your job description was particularly necessary for the smaller organisation, as job roles could evolve quickly. It also gave people a better appreciation of the challenges of other functions. I remember Tudor Brown once encouraging me to review a contract to ensure I understood its implications for my work. That gave me a much better appreciation of the legal department's work and, I hope, allowed me to work with them constructively on future projects.

At Arm's annual Organisational Development Conferences (later, Arm Leadership Conferences), one of the cultural consequences of this helpfulness caused some anxiety occasionally. Arm had often created a group to chase after a new type of business or acquired a company to help accelerate a strategy. When that new group presented their status and plans, people from all around the business would inevitably become very interested in how they were going about things – asking questions, trying to understand more, and looking for ways forward. On some occasions, this was welcomed. On other occasions, the newly acquired people were shocked, or at least surprised. Too much helpfulness, too quickly. One of Arm's significant challenges was to protect new entities from interference from the 'helpful' masses while navigating a path towards success. Acquisitions worked very effectively when an acquisition lead could pull the new team into the Arm way at the right pace. That meant a focus on culture as much as process. Ultimately that business unit needed to be contributing towards the bigger picture goals for Arm... else, why were they there?

Having a unified organisation encouraged helpfulness and, generally, a willingness to accept help when offered. This behaviour, in turn, helped spread knowledge, ideas, and good practice across the business. The result was better innovation and better business outcomes.

Cultural Drivers of Unity

Foundation Stones

The cultural legacy is a crucial factor in how Arm's togetherness evolved. The founding team's 'rugby team' attitude ensured that the different disciplines worked together toward common goals. They were also aware that they didn't have all the skills or resources needed to fulfil their goals, and so as new people were recruited, they too joined the team striving together to achieve the company goals.

Advanced RISC Machines was born into an uncertain, complex, and fast-changing environment – it would have been arrogant, at best, and foolish, at worst, for any early employees to believe they had all the answers. As a technology business in a rapidly evolving environment, it requires the combined brainpower of everyone to move in the right direction. The correct response to this environment is to include all voices and act with unity. And that's what Arm managed most of the time.

No Founders' Clique

In 1991 and 1992, the small team faced the extreme challenges of delivering new products for their investors and developing the business for new partners. They had no option but to work in a very open and collaborative manner if they were to succeed. The local business environment was not good at the time, and as Lee Smith told me, they had "no choice but to sink or swim together" (Smith L. , 2022). They chose to swim, knowing the goals needed to be achieved and forming close working relationships and strong friendships. However, what they did next was equally important: they welcomed new joiners into their fold.

The experience of joining the small but growing company was not of an unhealthy insiders' group which shared information and plans exclusively or resisted new people and their ideas. The feeling was that we were working together, original employees or new, as part of one organisation with a big challenge ahead. When I joined ARM in 1993, I quickly settled into a culture where I was welcomed as one of the 'gang', which felt very open and lacked the feeling of hierarchy. As I was early in my career, I never even considered that a small company would be any other way. Many years later, when comparing experiences with someone from another small company, I described ARM's culture and some of the reasons why I believed ARM was innovative. He reflected that in his business the handful of founders still exerted a powerful and outsized influence on the company. He felt they operated as a clique that discouraged 'outsiders' from feeling they could work at an equal level with them. Their founders almost certainly had good intentions, but it was the environment perceived by others that mattered.

For ARM, the feeling for people joining was: "Welcome to the gang, here's the goal, let's work at it together" – and without conscious thought, it's how we tried to treat later new joiners, too. We tried to welcome new people and ensure they felt part of the team – it was a default approach. Bruce Mathewson (long-term Arm® AMBA® architect) shared a story with me to illustrate this point (Mathewson, 2021). A few months after he joined in the mid-90s, he saw a new face in the kitchen, so automatically reached out a hand, introduced himself, and asked who the newcomer was and how long he'd been here. "Ten minutes – I'm the odd-job man fixing the fan," came the answer. Our default approach in action!

Robin gave some insight into how this may have come about. The 12 engineers already knew each other well, and he was determined to ensure that he joined them by mutual agreement. Robin wanted to ensure they wanted him to be the CEO and that he could work with them with as little hierarchy as possible. He also wanted everyone to play their part, hence requesting they all participate in the SWOT analysis in the first month. Robin knew he didn't have all the answers and so encouraged broad debate and challenge. Jamie Urquhart told me they spent a lot of time discussing strategy and plans and questioning everything together, in the office, over late-night curries or when travelling. Robin wanted to be the leader but knew that harnessing all ideas would be critical to their success. This attitude possibly helped inoculate the founding group from any kind of resistance to new joiners. Instead, we were welcomed as vital new people with skills and ambitions that would help drive them towards the collective goals.

> "Welcome to the gang, here's the goal. Let's work at it together"

Leadership Matters

Setting off with a clear direction and colleagues who pulled together is the easy part of growing an organisation. The challenge is maintaining that as the number of people increases, more offices open, and the company diversifies. ARM's IP licensing business naturally lent itself to the interconnectedness between business units, with the system IP supporting the processor IP, for example. However, it would have been easy to allow divergence from the feeling of unity with a broader range of product lines.

The attitude of leadership will make a massive difference to the ability to maintain unity across business groups. Does a group leadership team want to drive only their group's revenue growth or ARM's revenue growth? For ARM, the latter is what really mattered in the long term. Their mission needed to align with that ARM goal.

In 2004, ARM acquired Artisan Components, Inc for $913m, a provider of physical IP components for designing and manufacturing silicon chips (EETimes, 2004). The purpose was to increase the number of silicon IP products that ARM could sell, increase the number of customers, and generate better products through close collaboration. The group became the Physical IP Division (PIPD) within ARM. Silicon designers were free to use any physical IP they chose when implementing ARM's processor or system IP; likewise, a user of ARM's Physical IP offerings was free to use any processor or system IP they needed. Initially, the two businesses continued progressing together but without much apparent alignment. ARM needed to offer silicon designers benefits from using both ARM's processor and physical IP to achieve the acquisition goals. We also wanted PIPD colleagues to feel part of ARM and see the benefits of being one company.

The opportunity soon came for new leadership: Simon Segars took up the challenge to drive PIPD forward, with a clear focus on the bigger goals for the organisation. The division continued driving revenue through new physical IP licensing deals and increased royalties. They were also moving towards closer relationships with the Foundry manufacturers to ensure ARM was developing physical IP for the next-generation manufacturing processes. This would, in turn, give ARM better insights and knowledge to ensure the highest performance and power efficiency for the processor and system IP products. With Simon's ARM-focused leadership, ARM produced better products and revenue increased for PIPD. There was now clarity that the physical IP colleagues were part of the greater ARM community. The Arm® POP™[46] IP is one of the most tangible positive outcomes of the closer alignment, enabling the most efficient and highest-performance Arm processor cores implementations (Arm, 2022).

Conferences and Communication

If you want people to make good decisions and act proactively for the good of the business, then you need to ensure they have as much relevant information as possible. When there were fewer than 50 people in the rooms of the barn, this was easier to achieve than when ARM was over 5,000 people spread through 50 or so offices on almost every continent. Nonetheless, it's essential to start with the right culture. ARM chose openness as far as possible. There were regular communication meetings for the Cambridge offices, where we all gathered in an open plan area while members of the leadership team gave us the latest news on potential new customers and what we were learning from the market – telling their stories of unexpected cultural findings along the way. Post-IPO, these would often be wrapped up with the quarter's financial results and information

---

[46] Processor Optimized Package

on design wins. These meetings were an important way to keep people connected to the real business successes and fruits of their labour.

1996 – Fulbourn Road "Silver" building Comms meeting

Early on, we organised a weekly 'Lunch and Learn' for the silicon design group, where we invited someone outside the group to talk about their activity. It may have been directly relevant to the silicon group or indirectly relevant. It was always pleasing to see the level of interest and hunger to know more about ARM's business. This kind of activity may now be quite common in many organisations, but these events were crucial for ARM's collective learning and togetherness.

Perhaps less common was that ARM held many off-site conferences that, while smaller, almost everyone got to attend at least once per year. The stated purpose was to discuss critical areas of the business operations. Just as importantly, they were an opportunity for people from different groups and countries to get to know each other away from the office environment. ARM called these early conferences Global Operations Conferences (GOCs). They were an expensive but powerful way to cement and renew relationships and introduce new people to the cultural expectations of the company. They invariably involved a decent amount of free time in the evenings, allowing people to relax and get to know each other in the hotel bar and lounges – probably the most valuable part of the agenda.

As ARM grew, inevitably, we had more focused conferences: Global Sales Conferences (GSCs), Global Engineering Conferences (GECs), Organisational Development Conferences (ODCs), Arm Leadership Conferences (ALCs), regional GECs and ODCs, and so on. The culture of ARM being one of few barriers meant that these conferences were often over-subscribed by people outside of the intended audience. For example, everybody in marketing wanted to attend the sales conference. Likewise, everybody with any kind of technical or product role wished to participate in the engineering conferences, which had initially been for those in the product development groups only. After an infamous Global Sales Conference in Japan in 2000, which probably had more non-salespeople than sales, a tighter rein was put on the invite list for future years.

By 2018, the GEC had grown to over 500 people yet was only accommodating ~15% of the greater engineering community. Scaling is hard, but the culture had stuck – everyone wanted to be part of the relationship building and knowledge sharing; and the opportunity to debate any subject, especially if it was nothing to do with their group. Forming connections and relationships across country boundaries was especially valuable where product development projects were shared across the teams.

Operational Drivers of Unity

As well as creating suitable cultural mechanisms to promote and maintain unity, ARM was able to benefit from the necessity of collaboration across product groups. Where possible, ARM used these opportunities to promote 'joined up' solutions for customers, thus forcing alignment across business groups.

Technology Platforms

Significant steps forward in technology have often been great rallying cries within ARM, touching many areas of the organisation and demanding collaboration across groups. They have played huge roles in helping keep the one-company feeling alive. An example will help illustrate.

In the period 2010/11, ARM was developing several significant technologies as part of the competitive battle with Intel. ARM's goal was an extremely scalable computing system, including a new Mali™ graphics product supporting general-purpose compute. A lead partner had aggressive plans to be the first on the market with an SoC for the high-end mobile and tablet markets using this combination of ARM's technology. ARM was simultaneously developing the high-end Cortex®-A15™ CPU, the architecturally equivalent mid-range and low-power Cortex-A7™, the Mali-T604™ GPU, memory coherency IP, a 28nm Physical IP library, improved software tools, and several other related system IP products. The big-ticket software item was to support the Arm® big.LITTLE™ power management architecture that would dynamically switch between running software on either the faster Cortex-15 processor or the more power-efficient Cortex-A7. This architecture promised the highest responsiveness when demanded with the lowest power consumption. ARM needed to update and optimise the operating system kernel and several other components to support this capability. The programme was an ideal example of how big technology platforms required the involvement of many different business groups and engineering skills. This big challenge went a long way to ensure ARM's collective unity was upheld. The lead partner released their new SoC for their premium smartphone and tablet products, and the technology combination established clear power-efficiency benefits relative to ARM's competitors.

Technology Themes

As well as technology steps forward like the one described above, ARM has some overarching themes driving collaboration across the organisation on an ongoing basis.

One of ARM's most well-known technology themes is power efficiency. It all started with the original Acorn RISC Machine optimised to consume as little power as possible. From that point onwards, ARM's desire for power-efficiency across all its technology became a frequent rallying cry within the organisation as ARM diversified. In 2007, the term "Low-power Leadership" was coined as a driving force for innovation and cross-department collaboration. The mindset became well embedded – and was part of ARM's DNA. A demonstration of the multi-disciplinary impact of chasing power efficiency was the ARM® Intelligent Energy Management™ (IEM) technology first introduced with the ARM1176JZ-S™ processor in 2004. This processor supported implementations with different voltage domains on-chip and was supported by IEM-enabled system IP and software. The SoC designer then ensured the processor was using the lowest frequency and power possible, depending on the software performance needed. Engineers from the CPU design teams, system IP, software and physical IP groups worked together to provide a solution for the partnership. The technical challenge afforded by power-efficiency ensured that local goals were supplemented with ARM-wide objectives to ensure ARM's competitive position. It was a great driver of unity.

Outside Threats

The final area to highlight is the impact of outside forces. There is nothing like an external threat to promote togetherness and collaboration. Intel's assault on the mobile and tablet market with the x86 architecture galvanised Arm. The unofficial title of 'Fusion' represented a coming together of the different groups to fight a common foe. The company invested more quickly in higher performance processors and system IP, coordinated the combined efforts of the partnership in open source (Linaro) and generated unprecedented commercial interest in the introduction of Arm's 64-bit architecture. The increased focus and investment enabled Arm and the partnership to accelerate their high-performance developments. Arm-based CPUs are now a serious proposition in the server market, which was seen as a distant possibility when the activities started.

The impact of the 'Fusion' activity for Arm was far and wide, creating a sense of unity that was enhanced by the outside threat. This unity was enhanced even further by the very real sense that a large portion of the Arm partnership's market share could have been lost.

Chapter Summary and Lessons

During my 25 years at Arm and my subsequent consultancy in small companies, I have seen how important it is to have a coherent whole. The company goals should always trump local level goals – the bigger revenue prize is what matters most. That requires a top-down effort, ensuring business leaders have the right mindset and behaviours. With clear company-wide goals and challenges, collaborative and helpful behaviours should come to the fore. Arm was able to use multiple drivers to keep the spirit of unity alive. What lessons can be drawn from this?

1) **What's the North Star goal?** Find the easy to remember and understand, non-financial unifying goal for the organisation. Ideally, that goal will make a difference for industry, people, communities, or the environment. It should be identifiable and straightforward, allowing good decisions to be made when dealing with internal priorities and trade-offs.

2) **Take deliberate action to promote unity.** Minimise local incentives that work against the corporate whole. Appoint the right leaders and remove those who don't get it.

3) **Take opportunities as they arise.** Turn threats into opportunities and vigorously use them to promote cross-group interdependency and collaboration.

4) **Remember to never stop.** You're never too big to benefit from collaboration across borders and departments. If you have one compelling North Star, you are one company.

Afterword

As of mid-2022, the author is very aware of the twists and turns of Arm's current fate as a business wholly owned by Softbank Group. Nvidia called off its proposed acquisition of Arm in February 2022, and soon after, Softbank announced a plan to take Arm to an IPO, possibly in 2023. Then in March, Arm announced it would be reducing its workforce by around 15%.

None of this affects the basic premises behind this book. The period mainly covered is up to the Softbank acquisition in September 2016. Since then, the business has increased revenue, from $1.565bn in 2016 to $2.665bn in 2021. The number of Arm-based chip shipments has increased from 18bn in 2016 to over 29bn in 2021.

The business model is a very long-term one with a lot of momentum. The strength of the Arm technology and ecosystem makes it risky and expensive for semiconductor partners to use alternative CPU technology in many markets.

Nonetheless, I will finish by mentioning that there are significant challenges ahead for the organisation, not least the new competition of the RISC-V open source architecture. However, if Arm stays true to its core values of "We, not I", "Be your brilliant self", and "Passion for Progress", then I am sure it will be able to meet these challenges head-on and continue to grow and succeed.

Conclusion

I hope that it will now be clear why I chose the title of this book: "Culture Won". If I have not entirely succeeded in that mission, then let me end with a rallying cry for the power of culture in an organisation.

When I mentioned to ex-colleagues my intention of writing a book about Arm, there was a discussion about the many topics I could cover. However, one thing that united them all was the theme and importance of culture. As soon as I started talking about culture, there was almost immediate and enthusiastic agreement that this was the critical element that made the most significant difference for Arm. The collegiate working style, the willingness to debate, the desire to get things right, the absence of personal attacks or politics, and the clarity of purpose were strong drivers of success for Arm. We may not have always agreed on the best path forward, but we had confidence Arm would find the best way by listening to the market (and each other) and adjusting as needed as we progressed.

It all started with an agreed set of cultural statements, which Arm's founding team chose to complement the strategy and business model of the start-up. The culture evolved, of course, but the key elements vital to success were retained and codified. By making 'delivery' and 'behaviour' equally important at review time, Arm made it clear what it expected of people and encouraged managers to deal with counter-productive or damaging behaviours.

Whichever element of Arm's recipe for success you look at, it's clear that culture had a considerable role. Culture was at the heart of ensuring that Arm took the best decisions in most situations, most of the time. Whenever there was uncertainty, difficulty, or opportunities to be created or taken, 'Culture Won'.

Appendix: Industry and Technology Context

The semiconductor industry was already 25 years old when the first Acorn RISC Machine microprocessor sprang into life on 26th April 1985. Yet it was the "Goldilocks" moment for the technology that would form the foundation of Advanced RISC Machines. Arm's growth from the start-up of 12 people to a more than $1.5bn turnover in 2016 was a demonstration of just the right technology at just the right time with the right business strategy. But why was this the case?

"Moore's Law" of Semiconductor Scaling

The first working semiconductor transistor was demonstrated in 1947, but it was the 1959 invention of a type of transistor, the MOSFET, that effectively kick-started the semiconductor scaling revolution (Transistors, 2013). These transistors could be manufactured in an integrated circuit on a single semiconductor "chip" – usually silicon. Each transistor can either work as an amplifier or a switch. The latter allows digital logic circuits or storage devices to be created. As experience grew, the number of transistors that could be manufactured on each device multiplied. In his famous papers of 1964/5 (Moore, 1965), Gordon Moore showed how the number of MOSFETs transistors that could be economically manufactured on each integrated circuit already demonstrated a clear trend of doubling every 12 months. The trend he identified did indeed continue, albeit at a slightly reduced rate. The semiconductor scaling phenomenon has been forever known as "Moore's Law", despite being an observation and a prediction, not a law.

The semiconductor device fabrication process is a multistep sequence of photolithographic and chemical processing steps, during which the transistors and connections are gradually created on a wafer of semiconducting material (Semiconductors, 2022). The 'scale' of the process indicates the minimum feature size that can be manufactured – this was around 10μm in 1971, 1μm by the mid-1980s, and 5nm by 2020.

This shrinkage of minimum feature size has enabled an exponential reduction in cost per transistor and the increase in complexity of silicon devices. These improvements have, in turn, yielded massive increases in the capability of electronic equipment using the devices. The humble transistor is the most manufactured artefact in human history (13-sextillion, 2018).

The Computing Revolution

The history of computer development since the 1960s has been inextricably linked to the semiconductor industry. Computer design has taken advantage of the miniaturisation and performance improvements made possible by the increased number of smaller and lower-cost transistors.

The "mainframes" of the 1950s were joined by "mini" computers in the 1960s using integrated circuits. With further improvements to transistor integration, Large Scale Integration (LSI) chips matured to the extent that in 1971, Intel released the world's first complete computer on an LSI chip: the

"Microprocessor" was born (4004, 1971). This chip was designed for an electronic calculator, but its use was soon realised as a general-purpose engine. Microprocessors heralded a revolution in the size, cost, and accessibility of computer systems – now, hobbyists could join in, too. This accessibility led to the founding of multiple computer companies towards the end of the 1970s, including Apple Computers Inc. in the US and Acorn Computers Limited in Cambridge, UK.

Once it became possible to put tens of thousands of transistors on a highly affordable piece of silicon, called Very Large Scale Integration (VLSI), another significant step forward in microprocessor technology became achievable.

Reduced Instruction Set Computer (RISC)

From very early on in the development of digital computers, the program to be executed was stored in relatively small and slow external memory. So, computer architects sought to minimise the number of instructions needed to execute a program. The instructions themselves became more and more complex so that each one would "do more" – these were later called Complex Instruction Set Computers (CISC). Going the other direction, in 1974, a team led by John Cocke at IBM began work on a rack-based computer which deliberately reduced the number of instructions to simplify the design and allowed a more efficient implementation (Cocke, 1990). With the arrival of VLSI capability, the availability of lower-cost memory spurred a new way of thinking elsewhere, too. In 1980, a seminal paper was written using the term RISC for the first time (Patterson & Ditzel, The case for the reduced instruction set computer, 1980). RISC techniques were then used for many research and commercial microprocessor designs of the early 1980s and beyond. By reducing the number of instructions, the microprocessor's design could be simplified, and higher performance with better power efficiency achieved, so it was argued.

The researchers also found that the compilers which converted human-readable software programs into machine instructions tended to select a subset of those available anyway. So CISC microprocessors were not being fully utilised by the compilers, although they had an advantage in code density on paper. The RISC philosophy of computer design has stood the test of time, with almost all computers to this day using some of its concepts.

The Acorn RISC Machine (ARM)

When the Acorn team were looking to build a higher performance computer after the initial success of the BBC Microcomputer, they investigated many of the commercially available microprocessors. Being dissatisfied with what they found, they looked at the RISC options, but none were available commercially. So, they decided to start building their own in 1983, determined to use the RISC philosophy but focusing strongly on simplicity. By creating a very simple RISC microprocessor, they reasoned, they should be able to design and build themselves a high-performance but low-cost home and educational computer using the bare minimum of people and resources. So, for Acorn and Arm later, RISC meant high performance and power efficiency with low cost and low power.

The System on Chip Revolution

The SoC revolution is the final piece of the puzzle that helps set the context for Arm's opportunity to ride a wave of demand for microprocessor technology. By the early 1990s, transistors could now be manufactured at the sub-1µm scale, allowing the integration of a microprocessor, like ARM's, with system logic to build a complete system on a single device, the "System on Chip" (SoC, 2022). The ARM250 of 1992 integrated the latest version of the microprocessor, ARM2aS, with existing video, memory, and Input/Output (I/O) controllers to produce a single chip that was almost a complete home computer on a chip. Just add memory, display, keyboard, and I/O devices.

The SoC enabled a vast range of new applications to become viable, transforming many products into the digital ones we know today. Advanced RISC Machines' strategy was to license the microprocessor IP to semiconductor manufacturers who no longer needed their own microprocessor technologies to access these new markets. Licensable microprocessors opened substantial business opportunities for many new semiconductor vendors. They enabled whole new classes of consumer products powered by the low-cost, low-power, yet powerful microprocessors built into SoCs.

Glossary of Terms

Integrated Circuit – an electronic circuit formed on a small piece of semiconducting material, which performs the same function as a larger circuit made from discrete components

LSI – Large Scale Integration. Devices containing between 500 and 20,000 transistors

VLSI – Very Large Scale Integration. Devices with 20,000 to 1,000,000 transistors

Microprocessor – an integrated circuit that contains all the functions of a central processing unit (CPU) of a computer

CPU – Central Processing Unit

GPU – Graphics Processing Unit

DSP – Digital Signal Processor

I/O – Input and Output

4-bit – A processor able to execute operations on 4 bits of binary data simultaneously, i.e., 0 to 15 in decimal

8-bit – As above: 0 to 255

16-bit – As above: 0 to 65,535

32-bit – As above: 0 to 4,294,967,295

64-bit – As above: 0 to a ~1.845×10^{19}

MIPS – Millions of Instructions Per Second – an early and straightforward measure of CPU performance

References

13-sextillion. (2018). Retrieved from Computer History Museum: https://computerhistory.org/blog/13-sextillion-counting-the-long-winding-road-to-the-most-frequently-manufactured-human-artifact-in-history/

200bn. (2021, October 18). Retrieved from arm.com: https://www.arm.com/blogs/blueprint/200bn-arm-chips

4004. (1971). Retrieved from Intel: https://www.intel.co.uk/content/www/uk/en/history/museum-story-of-intel-4004.html

9201-Communicator. (2000, November 21). *the Nokia 9201 Communicator heralds the dawn of mobile multimedia*. Retrieved from Nokia: https://web.archive.org/web/20131212112345/http://press.nokia.com/2000/11/21/the-nokia-9210-communicator-heralds-the-dawn-of-mobile-multimedia/

Acorn RISCs it. (1987, June). *Popular Computing Weekly*. https://archive.org/details/popular-computing-weekly-1987-06-26/page/n4/mode/1up. Retrieved from https://archive.org/details/popular-computing-weekly-1987-06-26/page/n5/mode/1up

Active-Book. (1988). Retrieved from Computing history: http://www.computinghistory.org.uk/det/53902/Active-Book/

ARM. (1997). *Annual Report*.

ARM. (1998). *Annual Report*.

ARM. (2000). *Annual Report*.

ARM. (2001). *Annual Report*.

ARM. (2002). *Annual Report*.

ARM. (2003). *Annual Report*.

ARM. (2013). *Annual Report*.

ARM. (2015). *Annual Report*.

ARM. (2022). *A-Profile Architectures*. Retrieved from arm: https://developer.arm.com/architectures/cpu-architecture/a-profile

arm history. (2015, April 21). Retrieved from arm: https://community.arm.com/arm-community-blogs/b/architectures-and-processors-blog/posts/a-brief-history-of-arm-part-1

Arm-code-of-conduct. (2021). *Arm's Code of Conduct*. Retrieved from Arm: https://www.arm.com/company/code-of-conduct

ART. (1996, July). *Acorn RISC Technologies Brochure*. http://chrisacorns.computinghistory.org.uk/docs/Acorn/ART/ART_DS013_AcornRISCOS.pdf.

BBC Micro. (1981). Retrieved from BBC Micro 30th Anniversary: https://www.bbc.co.uk/news/technology-15969065

Biggs, J. (2021). (K. Clarke, Interviewer)

CACM. (2011, May). *Communications of the ACM*, pp. Vol. 54 No. 5, Pages 34-39. Retrieved from Communications of the

ACM: https://cacm.acm.org/magazines/2011/5/107684-an-interview-with-steve-furber/fulltext

Collins, J., & Porras, J. I. (2004). *Built to Last*. Harper Business.

Cooke, J. (1974). *RISC Architecture*. Retrieved from IBM.

Cortex-M. (2022). *Product selection*. Retrieved from https://www.arm.com/products

Curry, C. (2016, June 6). Chris Curry talks about Clive Sinclair, Sinclair Radionics and Acorn Computers. (J. Fitzpatrick, Interviewer) The Centre for Computing History. Retrieved from https://www.youtube.com/watch?v=KrTmvqwpZF8

Dyson-Various. (2022, January). Retrieved from Wikipedia: https://en.wikipedia.org/wiki/Dyson_(company)

Edmonson, A. C. (2019). *the fearless organization*. Wiley.

Engadget. (2011). *the Engadget interview arm co-founder John Biggs*. Retrieved from Engadget: https://www.engadget.com/2011-12-20-the-engadget-interview-arm-co-founder-john-biggs.html

English-Heritage. (1066). *Battle of Hastings*. Retrieved from English Heritage: https://www.english-heritage.org.uk/visit/places/1066-battle-of-hastings-abbey-and-battlefield/history-and-stories/what-happened-battle-hastings/

Flynn, D. (2021). Email and verbal. (K. Clarke, Interviewer)

Google. (2016). *Understand Team Effectiveness*. Retrieved from Rework. with google: https://rework.withgoogle.com/print/guides/5721312655835136/

Grisenthwaite, R. (2021, June 23). *Arm CCA will put confidential compute in the hands of every developer*. Retrieved from arm:

https://www.arm.com/company/news/2021/06/arm-cca-will-put-confidential-compute-in-the-hands-of-every-developer

Hauser. (2018). Retrieved from Archives IT: https://archivesit.org.uk/interviews/dr-hermann-hauser/

Hauser, H. (2014, June 20). Oral History of Hermann Hauser. (G. Hendrie, Interviewer) Retrieved from https://www.youtube.com/watch?v=Y0sC3lT313Q

Heffernan, M. (2014). *A Bigger Prize*. Simon & Schuster.

Honours. (2002). *2002 New Year Honours*. Retrieved from Wikipedia.

Howard, D. (2021). (K. Clarke, Interviewer)

IBM-Simon. (2012). *before iPhone and Android came Simon the first smartphone*. Retrieved from Bloomberg: http://www.businessweek.com/articles/2012-06-29/before-iphone-and-android-came-simon-the-first-smartphone

Imagination. (2022, January). *Imagination Technologies*. Retrieved from Wikipedia: https://en.wikipedia.org/wiki/Imagination_Technologies

Independent. (2016, March 7). *Business News*. Retrieved from Independent: https://www.independent.co.uk/news/business/news/google-workplace-wellbeing-perks-benefits-human-behavioural-psychology-safety-a6917296.html

Inglis, M. (2021). (K. Clarke, Interviewer)

Innovador. (2022, January 14). Retrieved from Innovador Consulting: www.innovador-consulting.co.uk

Intel. (2004, June 2). *Intel News Release*. Retrieved from intel: https://www.intel.com/pressroom/archive/releases/2004/20040601tech.htm

iPhone-sales. (2018). *Global Apple iPhone sales since fiscal year 2007*. Retrieved from Statista: https://www.statista.com/statistics/276306/global-apple-iphone-sales-since-fiscal-year-2007/

Jaggar, D. (2021). Emails. (K. Clarke, Interviewer)

Java. (1995, May 23). *JAVA TECHNOLOGY: THE EARLY YEARS*. Retrieved from sun.com: https://web.archive.org/web/20050420081440/http://java.sun.com/features/1998/05/birthday.html

KC LinkedIn. (2022, January 14). Retrieved from LinkedIn: https://www.linkedin.com/in/keith-clarke-22b4601/

Kimelman, P. (2021). Emails. (K. Clarke, Interviewer)

Linux. (1992). Retrieved from wikipedia: https://en.wikipedia.org/wiki/Linux

LWN. (2010, June). *Linaro seeks to simplify ARM Linux landscape*. Retrieved from lwn.net: https://lwn.net/Articles/391189/

Madrigal, A. C. (2013, May 16). *Paul Otellini's Intel: Can the Company That Built the Future Survive It?* Retrieved from The Atlantic: https://www.theatlantic.com/technology/archive/2013/05/paul-otellinis-intel-can-the-company-that-built-the-future-survive-it/275825/

Mathewson, B. (2021). Call. (K. Clarke, Interviewer)

Metzstein, S. (Director). (2009). *The Micro Men* [Motion Picture]. Retrieved from https://www.bbc.co.uk/programmes/b00n5b92

MIPS. (2022). *MIPS Technologies*. Retrieved from Wikipedia: https://en.wikipedia.org/wiki/MIPS_Technologies

Moore. (1965). Retrieved from Computer History: https://www.computerhistory.org/siliconengine/moores-law-predicts-the-future-of-integrated-circuits/

Nenni, D., & Dingee, D. (2015). *Mobile Unleashed*. SemiWiki LLC.

OHA. (2007, November 5). *Industry Leaders Announce Open Platform for Mobile Devices*. Retrieved from Open Handset Alliance: http://www.openhandsetalliance.com/press_110507.html

open-source, w. (2022). *History of free and open-source software*. Retrieved from Wikipedia: https://en.wikipedia.org/wiki/History_of_free_and_open-source_software

Overy, R. (1995). *Why the Allies Won*. Pimlico.

Palm. (2002). *Palm (PDA)*. Retrieved from Wikipedia: https://en.wikipedia.org/wiki/Palm_(PDA)

Patterson, D. A., & Ditzel, D. R. (1980). The case for the reduced instruction set computer. *ACM SIGARCH Computer Architecture News*, 25-33.

Patterson, D. A., & Sequin, C. H. (1982, September). A VLSI RISC. *Computer*, pp. Volume 15, Issue 9, pp 8–21.

PCW. (1997, September). *Personal Computer World – September 1997*. Retrieved from Computing History: http://www.computinghistory.org.uk/det/849/Personal-Computer-World-September-1997/

Peek, J. B. (1983). *The VLSI Circuitry of RISC I*. Berkeley: Computer Science Division, University of California, Berkeley.

Press Release. (1990). Retrieved from web archive: community. arm.com: https://web.archive.org/web/20160127093621/ https://community.arm.com/servlet/JiveServlet/previewBody/ 10926-102-1-22184/ARM_1st_Press_Release.pdf

R3000. (1988). Retrieved from Wikipedia: https://en.wikipedia. org/wiki/R3000

R380. (2000, November 24). *geek.* Retrieved from geek.com: https://web.archive.org/web/20110712081211/http:// www.geek.com/hwswrev/pda/ericr380/

Reuters. (2014, October 15). *Intel's quarterly results underscore challenge in mobile.* Retrieved from Reuters: https://www. reuters.com/article/us-intel-results-mobile-idINKCN0I40 0H20141015

RIM. (2011, August 3). *Research In Motion Introduces New BlackBerry 7 Smartphones.* Retrieved from rim.com: https:// web.archive.org/web/20120323091253/http://press.rim. com/release.jsp?id=5071

Saxby, R. (2021). Email and Verbal. (K. Clarke, Interviewer)

Semiconductors, W. (2022). *Semiconductor device fabrication.* Retrieved from Wikipedia.

Smith, A. (1776). *The Wealth of Nations.*

Stanford MIPS. (1983). Retrieved from Wikipedia: https:// en.wikipedia.org/wiki/Stanford_MIPS

Symbian. (1998, June). *Symbian Ltd.* Retrieved from Wikipedia: https://en.wikipedia.org/wiki/Symbian_Ltd.

Tesler, L. (1999). The Fallen Apple.

TOP500. (2021, June). Retrieved from top500.org: https:// www.top500.org/lists/top500/2021/06/

Transistors. (2013). Retrieved from Computer History Museum: https://computerhistory.org/blog/who-invented-the-transistor/

TrustZone. (2022). *Arm TrustZone Technology.* Retrieved from arm: https://developer.arm.com/ip-products/security-ip/trustzone

Tungsten. (2002). *Palm Tungsten.* Retrieved from Wikipedia: https://en.wikipedia.org/wiki/Palm_Tungsten

Turley, J. (2002). Retrieved from https://www.embedded.com/the-two-percent-solution/

Urquhart, J. (2021). Urquhart. (K. Clarke, Interviewer)

von Hippel, E. A., & von Krogh, G. (2009). Open Source Software and the 'Private-Collective' Innovation Model: Issues for Organization Science. *Organization Science,*, 3.

Wainwright, A. (1960). *Book Four – The Southern Fells.* Retrieved from https://www.walkupscafellpike.co.uk/lake-district-walk/scafell-pike-from-langdale/

Wilson. (2012). Retrieved from Computer History: https://www.computerhistory.org/collections/catalog/102746190

Wilson, S. (2021). Email. (K. Clarke, Interviewer)

WindowsCE. (1996). *Windows Embedded Compact.* Retrieved from Wikipedia: https://en.wikipedia.org/wiki/Windows_Embedded_Compact

Wozniak. (1977). Retrieved from Computer History: https://www.computerhistory.org/revolution/personal-computers/17/300#:~:text~Steve%20Wozniak%20designed%20the%20Apple,1979)%20made%20it%20a%20blockbuster.

About the Author

Keith Clarke was a geek who, aged 16, fell in love with the Acorn BBC Microcomputer in 1983. His father bought one for the family printing business and made a simple request, "Make it do the accounts," sending Keith on a journey learning to program and then to Southampton University, UK, where he studied Electronic Engineering, graduating in 1989. After some chip-design roles at an aerospace company and a brief time at Active Book Company's successor, EO Europe, in 1993, Keith joined the young Advanced RISC Machines as employee number 33.

If asked, Keith would say that the most surreal moment of his 25 years at Arm happened on his very first day at the company, when he was invited to a project meeting held standing next to a sheep field on a summer's day. After various engineering roles, Keith realised he was interested in helping others in the process of product development and became CPU Manager for the Cambridge group in 2000. With the company's explosive growth, by 2003, he found himself in the role of VP of Engineering, taking over from Simon Segars, who was moving to a commercial role on his journey towards CEO. Then from 2005 to 2018, Keith held various VP-level positions, including Technical Marketing, Business Unit Leader, Product Line Leadership, Programme Management, and finally, Operations (KC LinkedIn, 2022).

His pinnacle of satisfaction as an engineer came from adding the Arm® Thumb® technology to the ARM7™ microprocessor (and getting it right the first time). The high points of Keith's leadership journey came from managing teams delivering complex technologies under enormous timescale pressure and from helping partners develop products using Arm's technology.

Keith lives with his wife and boomerang children in a creaking 18th-century farmhouse in Cambridgeshire, UK.